Words *into* Action

Basic rights and the campaign against world poverty

Pat Simmons

Oxfam

(UK and Ireland)

Available in Ireland from Oxfam in Ireland, 19 Clanwilliam Terrace, Dublin 2. Tel: 01 661 8544

Published by Oxfam (UK and Ireland)
274 Banbury Road, Oxford OX2 7DZ

Designed by Oxfam Design Department OX326/PK/95

Printed by Oxfam Print Unit

Oxfam is a registered charity no. 202918

Contents

Acknowledgements

I would like to thank the following people for their help:

Kevin Watkins, whose *Oxfam Poverty Report* I have plagiarised frequently and at length; and Lindsay Judge, whose research on basic rights I have drawn on extensively.

My colleagues in Oxfam's Resources Unit, most of whom will recognise pieces of their own writing intertwined with mine.

Pedro Arias, who helped to prepare many of the statistical graphics.

The many staff in Oxfam's central and regional Campaigns offices, who made the time to discuss this book with me and to give me information, suggestions, reports, and photographs.

Dianna Melrose, and other Overseas Division staff, for advice and comments.

Colleagues in Oxfam's Photo Library, and Liz Clayton, for their help with photographs.

All the cartoons are from *Baobab,* a magazine produced by the Arid Lands Information Network, in Senegal.

Pat Simmons
Oxford, August 1995

The Oxfam Global Charter for Basic Rights

Every person has a basic right to:

a home

clean water

enough to eat

a safe environment

protection from violence

equality of opportunity

a say in their future

an education

a livelihood

health care

The Oxfam Campaign for basic rights is about turning words, and pious hopes, into action. It calls for a reaffirmation of the basic rights of every human being, because without these rights people will never be able to work themselves out of poverty, and the suffering it brings.

Demonstrating for democracy in Haiti.

Photo: Jenny Matthews

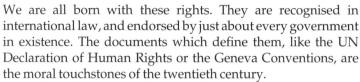

We are all born with these rights. They are recognised in international law, and endorsed by just about every government in existence. The documents which define them, like the UN Declaration of Human Rights or the Geneva Conventions, are the moral touchstones of the twentieth century.

But throughout the world, tens of millions of people continue to live in poverty, unable to claim their most basic rights. Poor people, and poor nations, are trapped in a vicious circle in which they remain poor because they cannot claim their basic rights, and forfeit those rights because they are poor.

The list of rights in Oxfam's Charter is not exhaustive. Most people would agree that there are other important rights: religious freedom, for example, or the right to freedom of speech. The rights highlighted in the Charter, however, represent those which Oxfam believes to be the most basic rights of all – to subsistence and security – without which other rights are unattainable.

Basic rights cannot be looked at in isolation. They are interrelated and interdependent. Where one is violated, others will be; successfully claiming one will make it easier to realise others. And where poor people are denied their rights, sooner or later we all suffer.

This book looks at some of the main obstacles which prevent poor people from claiming their basic rights and overcoming poverty. It calls upon the world's decision-makers — governments in both rich and poor countries, financial institutions such as the World Bank and the International Monetary Fund, the UN — to respect and protect these rights, and to work for a world in which all human beings can enjoy them, freed from the prison of poverty. It shows some of the triumphs, large and small, of poor people who are working to obtain their rights; and it outlines some of the ways in which their efforts have been made more effective by the support of people in the world's richer countries.

Poverty as we see it today in our affluent world is a savage violation of people's most basic rights. We hope that when you have read this book you will decide to take action, by becoming a part of the Oxfam Campaign, Together for Rights, Together against Poverty, to make those rights a reality. In doing so, you will be part of a movement for change which brings together people in poor and rich countries, who are working to bring about change in their own immediate communities, as well as trying to influence national and international policies.

The widening gap

- One in four of the world's people today lives in a state of absolute want:

  - they cannot afford the most basic shelter, or the minimum food requirements for leading an active, productive life.

- 35,000 children die every day because they are poor:

  - they lack the food they need to stay healthy
  - and their parents cannot afford basic health care for them.

- 130 million children do not attend primary school, 70 per cent of them girls:

  - their families are too poor to send them to school
  - and their governments have cut state education services.

- Half a million women die each year because they become pregnant

  - … and do not receive the health care they need before, during or after childbirth.

- 1.3 billion people have no safe water or sanitation

  - … and 80 per cent of all illness in the world is caught from drinking dirty water.

It's all too easy to see statistics like these, and the human suffering they hint at, as part of the natural order of human affairs — just "the way things are". Life has always been like this, after all; presumably it always will be. Perhaps the only sensible reaction is to be grateful we drew one of life's longer straws.

But there's nothing inevitable about this denial to millions of human beings of their most basic rights: the rights to food, clean water, health care, education, a livelihood.

- The world's governments jib at the $5 billion a year it would cost to provide basic education for all children. Yet they spend at least $800 billion a year on armaments.
- For just 16 per cent of what they currently spend on weapons, the world's poorest countries could meet the health and

education targets agreed at the 1990 World Summit for Children: these would include giving all children a basic education, reducing child deaths by a third, and providing clean water supplies for everyone.

- African governments currently spend more on repaying their debts to the World Bank, the International Monetary Fund, and other, richer, governments, than they do on the health and education of their citizens.
- In Latin America it would take only the equivalent of a 2 per cent income-tax increase on the wealthiest fifth of the population to raise the continent's poorest people above the poverty line.

The world can afford to wipe out poverty: we are choosing not to.

Instead, the gap between haves and have-nots — between the richest and poorest countries, the richest and poorest people within countries, between men and women within households — is stretching ever wider. And, in an increasingly prosperous world, millions of people are growing poorer.

Port-au-Prince, Haiti: the gap between rich and poor is increasing in most countries.

Photo: Jenny Matthews

Racing to fall behind

The gap between rich and poor countries is not just huge — it is also virtually bound to grow. Looking at the GNPs of two countries, one fairly affluent, the other fairly poor, reveals just how impossibly difficult it would be for a poor country to cross that gap.

Peru has a GNP per capita of $1,160; Norway's is $23,120. The gap between these two economies is so large that, if Peru's growth rate were identical to Norway's current 2.3 per cent and remained steady, it would take 95 years for it to reach Norway's present level. Meanwhile, of course, Norway would be likely to have become considerably richer. Even if the economy of Peru were to grow twice as fast as Norway's, its real income would still be falling steadily behind.

In fact, Peru's overall growth rate for 1965-90 was negative, at -0.2 per cent.

- In 1960 average incomes among the richest fifth of the world's population were 30 times greater than those of the poorest fifth. By 1990 the rich were receiving 60 times more.
- The combined wealth in 1994 of Mexico's 13 billionaires was more than double that of the 17 million poorest Mexicans. The number of billionaires is growing faster there than anywhere else in the world, while the proportion of the national income going to its poorest citizens is shrinking steadily.
- Despite continuing economic growth in the UK, the proportion of the population here with less than half the average income has trebled since 1977; the number of people living below the poverty line has soared from 5 million to nearly 14 million.

Unless we can start narrowing the poverty gap again, millions of people face a bleak future. By the end of this decade, on present trends, the number of Africans living in poverty will have grown by nearly a third, from 218 million to 300 million.

By the year 2025 there could be as many as 1.5 billion people living in severe poverty.

In Port-au-Prince, the capital of Haiti, more than 5,000 children live on the streets. Many of them are country children, driven to the city by desperate poverty.

Haiti is the poorest country in the Caribbean, and in all the Americas. The best land is used for sugar plantations; the rest is divided into small plots. Even on the steepest mountainsides, farmers try to grow maize and vegetables, and graze cattle and goats. The hillsides, once covered with trees, are now bare; rain washes away the soil, leaving only bare rock in some places. Over the years the trees have been cut down to build homes and provide fuel for cooking.

High taxes and land rents, poor crop yields, and low prices, make it almost impossible to earn a living and bring up a family. Families buckle under the impossible tensions, and many of the casualties finish up on the streets of Port-au-Prince and other cities. Some of Haiti's street children are only five years old. Though many maintain links of a sort with their families, they must scratch a living for themselves in the city as best they can. With no clean water to drink or wash in, very little food, and no health care when they fall ill, they are constantly harassed by the police and army, who see them as young criminals. Deprived of education or training, marginalised, and excluded from any positive role in society, they are unlikely to be able, in their turn, to provide physical or emotional security for their own children.

This street child receives help from a local community organisation.

Photo: Jenny Matthews

Violent clashes over land in Kenya have resulted in the displacement of thousands of people. Since 1991 up to 300,000 smallholder farmers have had to desert their homes and land, for the temporary security of missions, churches, and school houses.

Anthony and Gaudensia Obon'go are the innocent victims of political power struggles that exploit ethnic differences, and set people against each other.

"I live at the edge of the village. I heard the dogs barking at one o'clock in the morning, and went outside," says Anthony. "There were men armed with spears and arrows. As I ran to my neighbour, I was hit. I fought off my attackers but then collapsed."

Anthony was in hospital in Kisumu for nine days. When he and Gaudensia returned home, the place was deserted. "My house and sheds had been destroyed. All were burned, along with the sugar cane, and the heat from the fire had scorched the orange trees. And the school was burnt down. It was just like the bush."

Unable to salvage any belongings, Anthony and Gaudensia followed other villagers to Muhoroni, a few kilometres away. They took refuge in a mission, and were given food, blankets, and plastic sheeting.

After six months they returned home. Before the attack on their village, they had been successful farmers. Now, their resources all gone, they had to work hard to rebuild their ruined house and replant the crops and trees which had been destroyed.

Anthony and Gaudensia have a home once more, but thousands of Kenyans are still displaced.

Anthony and Gaudensia cultivating their land.

Photo: Geoff Sayer

The vision that faded

"Never again." Two simple words, expressing the longing of an entire generation: a generation which had witnessed not just the darkness of the Second World War, but the preceding decades of economic depression and blighted human lives.

Half a century or so ago, the United Nations and institutions like the World Bank and the International Monetary Fund came into being as an expression of that longing. Never again must violence and conflict be allowed to destroy the lives of the world's people. Never again were poverty and mass unemployment to be tolerated.

The UN Charter and the Universal Declaration of Human Rights* provided the moral framework for a new system of rights and obligations upon which this new order was to be built. These visionary documents recognised that human beings have a range of basic rights. They outlined the realisation of those rights as the way to combat poverty and reduce conflict. And they placed responsibility for protecting them upon the world's governments.

According to President Roosevelt, this was "no vision of a distant millennium," but "a definite basis for a world attainable in our own time and generation". The world as we approach the end of the millennium looks rather different. Increasingly, the power of transnational corporations (TNCs) rivals that of nation states. Most economic reforms of the past couple of decades have concentrated almost solely on deregulating markets to the benefit of the TNCs; they have ignored the need to ensure that as many people as possible are able to benefit from the wealth created by deregulation.

Even as governments have abandoned much wasteful and unnecessary intervention, they have also begun to shirk their duty to regulate their economies in the interests of poor people, and to invest sufficiently in health and education services. They have reneged on their commitment to deliver the rights they have already signed up to.

Since 1948 the rights articulated in the Universal Declaration have been consolidated in other international legal instruments and declarations, which all reaffirm on paper the rights of

* see page 107

individual human beings to a livelihood, health care, and enough to eat; more and more, at both global and national levels, these rights are being ignored and undermined.

Poverty, and the denial of rights associated with it, is morally wrong. It is a human creation, and, given the political will, it can be tackled and done away with. It is also economically inefficient, and damaging in the end to everyone, rich as well as poor.

All too often, rising poverty gives rise to violent conflict, refugee crises, increased crime, and trade in narcotic drugs: all problems that do not respect borders and from which the better off cannot insulate themselves. "Security for the few," in the words of Nelson Mandela, "is insecurity for all."

Fifty years ago, Oxfam came into being in response to the plight of civilians like this little girl, facing hardship and starvation in Nazi-occupied Greece.

Photo: Oxfam

Stacking the odds against the poor

Brave new world

The five decades which have elapsed since the UN was founded have seen some remarkable changes. Global economic wealth has increased sevenfold, and average incomes have tripled. Overall, people are living longer, fewer children are dying, more children are attending school.

The partnership between modern technology and global markets has been a powerful and successful one, which has given millions of people increased prosperity and security. It really begins to seem perfectly feasible for every individual to claim the rights that he or she was born to, and to live a full life, free from poverty.

Material prosperity is increasing even in many very poor countries.

Source: *World Development Report 1994*

a Bolivia b Honduras c Nepal d Rwanda

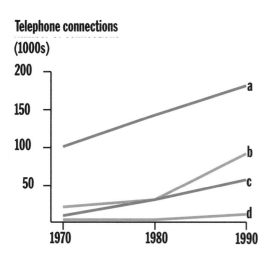

Telephone connections

(1000s)

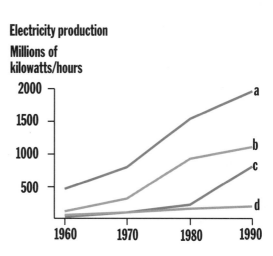

Electricity production

Millions of kilowatts/hours

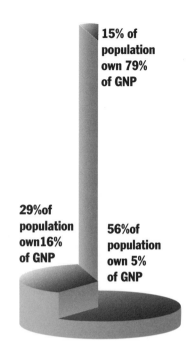

15% of
population
own 79%
of GNP

29%of
population
own16%
of GNP

56%of
population
own 5%
of GNP

Source: World Bank *Social Indicators of Development 1993*

State investment has helped to fund Singapore's economic "miracle".

Photo: Jeremy Hartley

But what do we see instead if we look at the world around us? Armed conflict wrecking the lives of millions of men, women, and children. And — as often as not entwined in a lethal partnership with such conflict — the "silent holocaust" of poverty. Imagine every UK child under 16 suddenly dropping dead — each year an equivalent number of children in poor countries die as a direct result of poverty. Each one of these deaths is preventable.

In a world which has put men on the moon, and can shift money in seconds from London to Tokyo to New York, children still die from drinking dirty water, and one person in four cannot meet their most elementary needs. Millions more people live on the edge of an abyss, uncertain where tomorrow's food will come from — or whether it will come at all. Unable to save, or break out of the poverty in which they are trapped, they are acutely vulnerable to drought, conflict or the introduction of user charges for basic health and education services.

Economics for people

The financial institutions and systems set up after the Second World War (the World Bank and the International Monetary Fund) were intended to provide a foundation for shared prosperity. A free flow of goods and money would be central to creating and spreading wealth. On the other hand, there would be measures in place to keep this flow under control. In the past, uncontrolled markets had been associated with poverty, inequality, and instability: these evils were to be avoided in the post-war world by making markets work, at national and global level, for the benefit of as many people as possible.

Today, however, most governments and financial institutions have moved firmly over to a belief in non-interventionist economic policies. Countries such as Korea and Singapore (two of the South-East Asian "tigers") have built their miracle economies with the help of high levels of state intervention, major redistributions of assets, and heavy investment in basic health and education services. Nevertheless, the formula now is for deregulated markets, dismantled trade barriers, and reduced state subsidies and investment. Such a formula, it is intended, will create wealth for the relatively few, which will then trickle gradually down to the many, enabling some of the benefits of growth to reach the lowest strata of every society.

In reality, the rich are becoming richer, while huge numbers of the poor become poorer. One-fifth of the world's people, living in the poorest fifty countries, now receive between them less than 2 per cent of global income.

World trade

Since the war, international trade flows have increased by a factor of 12, to over $4 trillion. Many countries depend heavily on these flows: on average, middle-income countries now obtain a third of their national incomes from such trade, and even the poorest countries depend on it for a quarter of their income.

But increasingly, the rules of the international trade game favour the world's rich countries over its poor ones. And in the past couple of decades a new breed of winner has emerged: the powerful transnational corporation.

The "free market" today is largely dominated by a handful of private companies. The 100 largest TNCs control over one-third of all foreign investment, and 40 per cent of world trade now takes place within TNCs. General Electric, General Motors, and Ford between them control assets worth roughly double Mexico's entire gross domestic product.

As more and more countries are pressurised into abandoning restrictions on movements of capital, and as modern technology makes it possible to move money rapidly in and out of countries, the TNCs are becoming ever more mobile and so more powerful. National boundaries and economic policies are becoming almost irrelevant to them.

In fact, measures aimed at protecting the livelihoods, health, and future of poor people — laws on minimum wages, workers' rights, and working conditions, anti-pollution measures, environmental protection — are under attack, as TNCs move production and jobs from one country to another in a restless search for minimum restraint and maximum profitability. The resulting pressure for an ever-lower common denominator affects rich and poor countries alike, as job opportunities are shifted from rich countries to poorer countries, and then, as workers in those countries start to demand slightly higher wages, to still poorer ones. In some cases, the TNCs themselves offer better wages and conditions than local employers, but push down the rates they pay local suppliers, who, in their turn, push down the wages they pay their own work-forces.

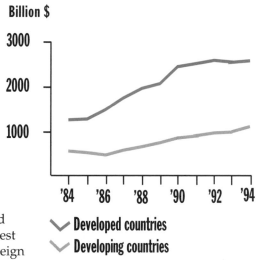

Value of exports

Source: GATT, *International Trade, 1993: Statistics*

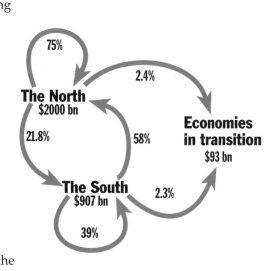

The world's trade flows

Source: UNCTAD

15

Rule 3

Overproduce and undercut

The EU's Common Agricultural Policy (CAP) subsidises production by European farmers and, when that production leads to surpluses, subsidises exports. The recently concluded Uruguay Round of the General Agreement on Tariffs and Trade (GATT) did little to change this

Rule 4

Stitch up the South

The Multi-fibre arrangement (MFA) protects Northern textile industries from cheaper Third World imports. Under the MFA Northern countries impose quotas on Third World textile producers, but not on other Northern producers. The MFA is temporary — in operation since 1974, it will be phased out by 2005!

11 Rich industrialised countries impose escalating tariffs, charging more on your processed goods than on the raw materials
Go back two squares

World Bank experts advise you to clear forested hillsides: sell the timber, and plant cash crops.
12 *Go forward one square*

13 Heavy rain washes soil from the hill-sides and causes floods.
Go back two squares

Get a new foreign expert to advise you.
Go forward one square

14

Try to add value to your commodities by doing some of the processing yourself.
Go forward one square. **10**

The Trade

A Game every developing country must play

Farmers, ruined by the low grain prices, abandon their farms and migrate to the cities looking for work.
See Rule 3
9 *Go back two squares*

8 Cheap grain from the EU floods your markets. Urban food buyers are happy.
Go forward one square

As a former European colony you may be eligible to join Lomé.
See Rule 2 *Go forward two squares*
7

6 Flooding destroys rival producers' crops. Prices go up.
Go forward two squares

Rule 2

Lucky for some

The Lomé Convention regulates trade between the European Union (EU) and the African Caribbean and Pacific (ACP) group of countries. It gives ACP countries preferential access to the EU market, and protection against falling commodity prices.

Rule 5

Make more rules

The World Trade Organisation (WTO) was established in 1995 as a successor to GATT. Its scope and powers are wider than GATT's, but it comes no closer to addressing many of the long-standing problems faced by most poor countries in the world trading system. Discriminatory trade policies, subsidised agricultural exports, and low prices for the commodities they produce will continue to undermine the livelihoods of most people in poor countries

19 WTO is dominated by rich industrialised countries.
Go back to Square One

Whatever you do, the rules seem to be stacked against you. Join WTO to try to change the rules.
See Rule 5   **18**

15 Go into textile manufacturing, taking a lead from Taiwan and Korea.
Go forward one square

Rich industrialised countries impose textile quotas under the MFA.
See Rule 4
Go back one square   **16**

17 Beet sugar exports from the EU, subsidised by the CAP, undermine your sugar cane exports, leading to low prices.
Go back one square

The Trade Game

Rule Book

The rules will change constantly during play

Game

Maybe there's strength in numbers — join UNCTAD
See Rule 1
5

4 Diversify into other commodities to spread the risk
Go forward one square

Other countries do the same and the price collapses.
Go back to Square One
3

2 Experts from rich industrialised countries advise you to increase exports of your main commodity to bring in more money

Rule 1

Stall 'em

UNCTAD — United Nations Conference on Trade and Development — was established in 1962 to promote international trade and commerce with a principal focus on the problems of developing nations. Its influence is limited to a research and advisory role.

Square One

You are a poor country and you want to develop.

Price fluctuations for coffee
(top) and cocoa (below)
projected to the year 2000
Source: World Bank

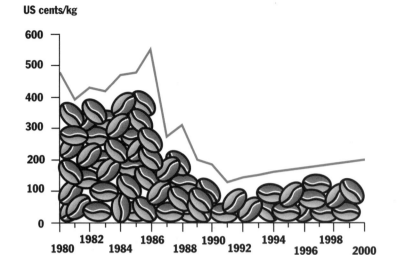

US cents/kg

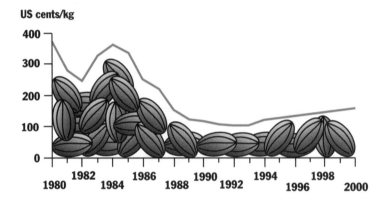

US cents/kg

UK newspapers in early 1995 reported the complete transfer of a large UK plastic-bag factory to China. Machinery and equipment were simply packed up and flown out. The UK factory workers were kept on for a while to train the Chinese workers who were to take their jobs; then they were laid off.

In South-East Asia, Japanese investment has moved in the last few years to Malaysia and Thailand, where wages are one-tenth those that Japanese firms had been paying in South Korea and Taiwan. Now enter Vietnam, where, since the economy was opened to foreign investors in the mid-1980s, people have been eager to work for still less than their Malaysian and Thai counterparts. However Japanese investors may decide to respond to the arrival of this new, and highly educated, work-force, one fact is clear: workers in poor countries lose out, from low wages and poor working conditions because of the erosion of workers' rights, while the rich in both poor and rich countries benefit.

Free trade contains perils enough for poor countries, but, in fact, trade is far from "free" for them: the rules of the game have been drawn up by the winners. The need for "a level playing field" is often stressed by policy-makers from the rich industrialised countries, stressing the virtues of the free market. In fact, the benefits of international trade are currently strongly skewed towards the countries of the rich, industrialised world. They insist on open markets for their products, while at the same time maintaining trade barriers to protect their own industries from competition. In agricultural production, for example, the level playing field runs all the way downhill from the heavily subsidised farms of Europe and North America, to the staple-food systems of Asia, Africa, and Latin America.

At present, about one-fifth of all exports from poorer countries face an array of protectionist barriers which discriminate specifically against them. The Multi-Fibre Arrangement, for example, scheduled to remain in place for another ten years, sets limits on exports of textiles and clothing from developing countries.

It costs those countries about $50 billion a year in lost export earnings, roughly equivalent to the total flow of development aid to all poor countries from the richer countries who are making it impossible for them to export their goods.

Even without these arbitrary controls, rich countries hold the whip hand. Local crop prices in many poor countries are being depressed, and people's livelihoods undermined, by the "dumping" of heavily subsidised food exports from rich countries. In 1991 alone, for example, the European Union shipped 54,000 tons of beef to West Africa. Subsidised by European tax-payers, the meat sold at 50 per cent below the price of locally reared beef. The results for a country like Mali, where trade in animals accounts for 30 per cent of all exports, have been disastrous. "The European Union is giving us money to help us develop," commented a government trade officer, "but at the same time they are preventing us from trading with our neighbours."

Livestock market, Mali.
Photo: Jeremy Hartley

The debt trap and its consequences

In 1994 over four-fifths of Uganda's export earnings — $162 million — went on debt and interest payments. By comparison, it was able to spend a total of only $120m on health and education services.

For some 15 years, many of the world's poorest countries have been trapped in debts which they are unlikely ever to be able to repay. Interest rates have increased, world prices have fallen for the commodities they depend on to pay those debts, and they are, to all intents and purposes, virtually bankrupt.

Most have had to turn to the World Bank and the International Monetary Fund for help, for new loans to meet the interest payments on their existing loans. As a result, the two institutions now wield considerable power in many poor countries, and have been able to demand major adjustments to the economic policies of their governments.

The Structural Adjustment Programmes (SAPs) that governments have had to adopt, to qualify for an IMF rescue-package, have emphasised reducing public expenditure, and market deregulation, at the expense of measures to enhance the rights of poor women and men. According to both institutions, SAPs have provided frameworks for sustainable economic recovery, if at some short-term cost to some individuals.

Certainly, there was a need for economic reforms, but these should have been designed to address the needs of poor people. Poor men and women, however, were never consulted about what the changes might mean for their lives. In their eyes, higher interest rates have meant that small producers cannot obtain the credit they need, that wages have fallen dramatically, and employment become highly insecure. Women are carrying a particularly heavy burden, as they struggle to make ends meet, and compensate for reductions in state services.

The World Bank itself has become concerned about the impact on poor people of cuts in state spending. It now aims, so far without much obvious success, to ensure that essential state services are protected in new adjustment programmes. But there is a huge gap between rhetoric and good intentions on the one hand, and what is actually happening out in the villages and squatter settlements on the other. The last five years have seen, for example, Zimbabwe reducing its spending on primary health care and basic education services by a third, the Zambian education budget pushed down to its lowest-ever level, and Pakistan's health budget declining from 1 per cent to 0.7 per cent of gross domestic product.

Where state services survive, they now often have to be paid for, either up-front or through charges for a whole range of essential "extras", such as pencils, contributions to school repair funds, or medicines. So fewer children learn to read and write, and fewer

External debt: developing countries 1970-94

Source: *Vital Signs 1995*

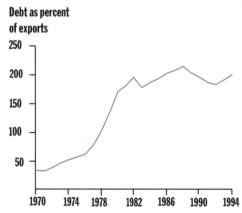

Debt as percent of exports

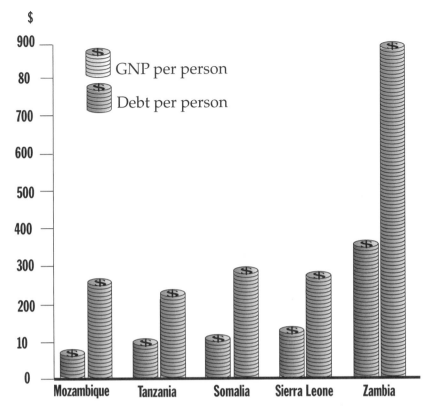

$

900	
80	
700	
600	
500	
400	
300	
200	
10	
0	

GNP per person

Debt per person

Mozambique   Tanzania   Somalia   Sierra Leone   Zambia

Left: Debt and GNP per person in selected countries
Source: *World Guide 1995*

Below: Classroom in Zambia, 1990. Even before recent cuts in education spending, Zambian schools were overcrowded and under-resourced.
Photo: Chris Johnson

women get the antenatal care they need: in Zimbabwe in 1994 the number of babies born to women who had had no antenatal treatment rose from 1.6 per cent to nearly 9 per cent; and those women were five times more likely to die during or just after childbirth. Fortunately, the Zimbabwean government has come to recognise the harm being caused by the new policies, and has withdrawn fees for rural health services.

Essential though many of the enforced reforms were, there has been far too little attempt to help poor people share in any resulting increase in prosperity. Unless they are enabled to participate in the new markets opening up, for example by being given access to land and affordable loans, they are likely to suffer rather than benefit as a result of market deregulation. Their poverty is likely to be significantly reduced only if they have a say in critical decisions which will have far-reaching effects on their lives: their experience and perceptions must be taken into account in the design of national economic policies.

Maternal deaths in Zimbabwe compared with Ministry of Health recurrent expenditure per person, 1987-92

Source: UNICEF

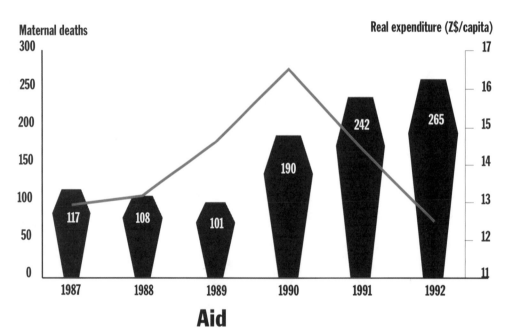

Aid

Of all the aspects of the relationship between high- and low-income countries, aid is probably the one with the most myths around it. In the UK, public perception tends to be that we are sending huge sums of money — money that we can ill afford — to help poor people in poor countries. At least until the Pergau Dam affair hit the media, aid was often seen as a gift from "us" to "them", the product of generosity and compassion. If the generosity had strings attached, that was, and still to some extent is, seen as only reasonable.

In many ways, the myths exaggerate the importance of aid. In

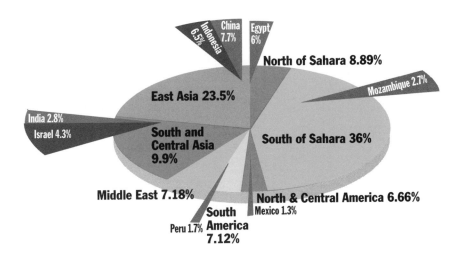

China 7.7%
Indonesia 6.5%
Egypt 6%
North of Sahara 8.89%
Mozambique 2.7%
East Asia 23.5%
India 2.8%
Israel 4.3%
South and Central Asia 9.9%
South of Sahara 36%
Middle East 7.18%
North & Central America 6.66%
Mexico 1.3%
Peru 1.7%
South America 7.12%

Distribution of net development aid from major donor countries 1989–93

Source: OECD

fact, the governments of rich countries would do far more for human welfare than they achieve through their aid budget, if they simply wrote off some of the debts owed to them, or ceased to operate double standards in demanding access to poor country markets, while putting up trade barriers to their own.

Nor are the sums of money involved particularly massive. The target set by the UN for aid budgets is 0.7 per cent of GNP. A modest enough target, but one that has so far been met by only four countries. Indeed, most countries are now moving further away from it. 1993-94 saw deep cuts in bilateral (government-to-government) transfers of aid. The 21 OECD countries reduced their aid budgets by over 6 per cent in real terms, with aid grants to non-African countries falling by 25 per cent. The US, already one of the countries furthest from meeting the UN target, reduced its aid expenditure by 19 per cent. Canada's overseas aid is expected to fall to 0.3 per cent of GNP by 1997-98; over a period which has seen its defence budget cut by 4.9 per cent, its aid budget has fallen by 15 per cent.

Overall, in 1993-94, the rich industrialised countries spent just 0.3 per cent of their GNP in aid, the lowest level recorded for two decades.

If the popular myths are mistaken about the size of the rich world's aid budgets, there is still more misunderstanding about the impact they are designed to make in reducing poverty.

For a start, resources are not concentrated in the countries where they are most needed. According to the UNDP, the poorest 40 per cent of the population of the developing world receives less than half the aid that goes to the richest 40 per cent.

Aid tends to be targeted at the countries of most strategic importance. Between them, for example, Israel and Egypt absorb over half the US aid budget, receiving over \$5bn annually: three

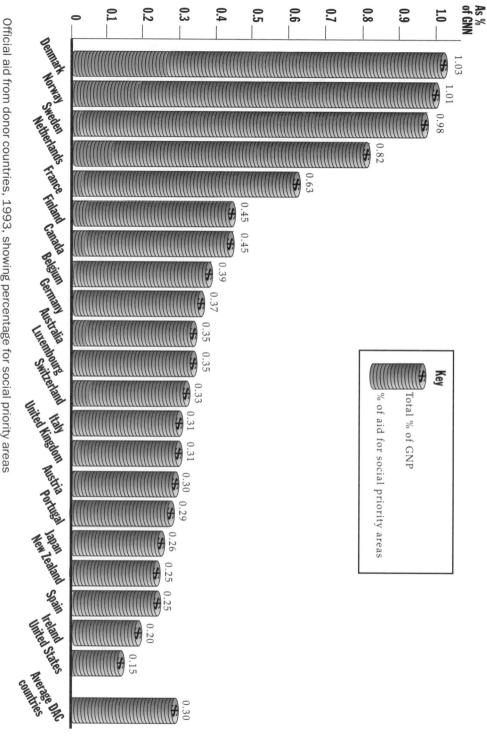

As %
of GNN

Denmark — 1.03
Norway — 1.01
Sweden — 0.98
Netherlands — 0.82
France — 0.63
Finland — 0.45
Canada — 0.45
Belgium — 0.39
Germany — 0.37
Australia — 0.35
Luxembourg — 0.35
Switzerland — 0.33
Italy — 0.31
United Kingdom — 0.31
Austria — 0.30
Portugal — 0.29
Japan — 0.26
New Zealand — 0.25
Spain — 0.25
Ireland — 0.20
United States — 0.15
Average DAC countries — 0.30

Key
Total % of GNP
% of aid for social priority areas

Official aid from donor countries, 1993, showing percentage for social priority areas

Source: Word Bank

times the US aid budget for the whole of sub-Saharan Africa. Israel receives $626 per person: Peru, where average incomes are one-twelfth of those in Israel, only $30 per person.

Even where aid is spent in poor countries, it does not always benefit the poorest people. Between them, bilateral donors spend only 7 per cent of their budgets on areas such as primary health care, basic education, water and sanitation provision, and nutrition programmes.

Even the money which does go on health and education services tends to benefit the better off: about a third of British aid is spent on priority areas like health and education, but four-fifths of its 1992 aid budget for education went on universities, technology centres, and secondary education, rather than on primary education. Four times as much aid worldwide goes on water supplies and sanitation for urban areas as for rural areas, much of it being used to provide relatively high-cost tap water to private homes. The primary health care facilities which could prevent or treat 80 per cent of the diseases afflicting poor people, receive only 1 per cent of international aid spending. Most donors continue to fund teaching hospitals, which provide high-cost services to urban populations.

The pursuit of commercial self-interest also reduces the effectiveness of aid programmes in combating poverty. Most aid donors use part of their aid budgets to promote exports by their own industries: around 75 per cent of British aid is tied to the purchase of British goods and technical assistance. In fact, in some cases, the aid budget is used to subsidise the British commercial sector by helping firms with the costs of tendering for projects.

Because the tying of aid insulates donors from competitive pressures, developing countries end up paying above the market rate for goods and services. One recent estimate suggests that these extra costs to aid recipients represent more than 15 per cent of the aid provided. According to the World Bank, untying all aid donations would be worth as much as $4bn a year to developing countries: more than the entire UK aid budget.

It could also result in more appropriate solutions to people's problems, because developing countries would be able to acquire what they need, rather than what donor countries have available to sell them. It might enable people to develop their own skills,

Sidy L. DRAME

rather than having foreign "experts" foisted on them: of the $12bn or so of development aid spent annually on training, project design, and consultancy, over 90 per cent goes on such experts. This is not just a waste of the potential of people in poor countries; it is also only too likely to lead to bad advice being given by people with insufficient understanding of local situations.

The Pergau Dam scandal illustrated everything that is wrong with tied aid. The largest programme ever financed under the Aid Trade Provision of the UK aid programme, it cost some £234m. An ODA report concluded that it was an expensive and inefficient source of power, and "a very bad buy" for both Malaysian consumers and British tax-payers. But the deal had been pushed through because it was linked to billions of pounds of British exports to Malaysia, including over $1bn of arms exports.

Ecological footprints

Land is constantly washed away from Hatiya Island, Bangladesh, particularly during storms in the Bay of Bengal.

Photo: Shahidul Alam

The damage being done to our environment affects us all, and is likely to impoverish all our lives if it continues unchecked. But global environmental problems, such as the warming effect of "greenhouse" gases, pose particular problems for poor people.

For example, impoverished Bangladeshi families, left destitute by the 1991 Bay of Bengal cyclone, have won the right

to cultivate small pieces of land on Hatiya Island. In reality the island is little more than a low-lying sandbar created by siltation — only people with no other options would even consider trying to live there. Nevertheless, the island's new community is struggling to protect its new home, by building embankments and planting trees. They are developing all manner of ways of making a livelihood from their perilous environment. All their initiatives will count for little, however, if global warming causes a rise in sea-level, and increases the frequency and intensity of flooding.

Throughout the world, poor people are the most immediately threatened by global environmental degradation, since so many of them live in fragile ecological areas and lack the resources to protect themselves. Yet it is the rich — nearly all of us in the developed world, and the elites of poorer countries — who are responsible for most of it. The industrialised world has largely caused the build-up of carbon emissions which threatens to lead to global warming, but it is poor people, like those on Hatiya Island, who will suffer.

The poor are often blamed for the threat to the global environment because, it is said, they have "too many" children, and therefore put damaging pressure on land and resources. This accusation overlooks the fact that poverty usually cuts people off from the very family-planning services the rich world blames them for not using. Or that, with no social security or pensions, and with so many children dying young, it can be a rational choice for poor people to have large families as security for their old age.

O. DIAKHITE

In any case, it is poverty, rather than "over" fertility, which most frequently forces men and women to degrade their local environment: squeezed out on to poor, unproductive land, many families have to sacrifice tomorrow's environment for today's meal or this year's harvest. Many of them have no realistic choice but to over-cultivate their land, over-graze their pastures or cut down their forests for firewood.

Whatever damage they may do, however, is minute compared with the havoc wrought by the rich. The average American, for example, has an environmental impact on the planet about 140 times greater than the average Bangladeshi, and 250 times greater than the average African. With only 16 per cent of the world's population, the industrialised countries generate nearly 70 per cent of its industrial waste and over 30 per cent of the gases responsible for global warming.

The agenda of the 1992 Rio Earth Summit was defined to a great extent by the interests of the industrialised world, and concentrated most sharply on the actions which poor countries should take. Attempts to make the rich, industrialised world clean up its act, such as the Climate Change Convention, commit governments to little effective action: targets and timetables are left vague. For President George Bush, "the American lifestyle is not up for negotiation", a view tacitly shared by the governments of most rich, industrialised nations and almost guaranteed to lead to a steadily worsening environmental situation. We are all likely to suffer when that happens, but, almost certainly, it will be poor people who suffer first, and most.

Conflict

Nothing violates people's rights more massively than war and armed conflict. For the time being, the old model of conflicts between states has largely given way to one of conflicts within states, but the results are similar: 40 million people left as refugees or internally displaced within their own countries; a million people killed in Rwanda in 1994; a quarter of a million killed in Bosnia and 2.5 million driven from their homes.

War today is waged mainly against non-combatants: four out of every five casualties are civilians, most of them women and children. According to UNICEF, 1.5 million children were killed in conflict between 1982 and 1992, and another 4.5 million left disabled. In some conflicts, rape has become a routine way of terrorising and humiliating women, and, often, through them, their entire ethnic group.

Even in times of peace, conflict continues to claim victims. There are up to 110 million anti-personnel mines scattered across the world, mostly lying in the fields and roads of poor

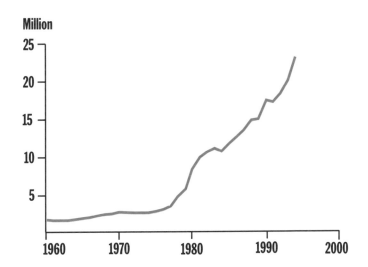

Million

Number of refugees worldwide 1960–94

Source: *Vital Signs 1995*

countries. Every day they kill over 20 people, and injure double that number. The indirect damage they cause is long-lasting and almost as harmful. Good land has to be left uncultivated, often in areas where people are going hungry. Travelling or transporting goods along mined roads remains fraught with danger, leaving communities isolated, and jeopardising attempts to rebuild war-wrecked economies.

Rwandan refugees walking towards Katale camp, Zaire.

Photo: Howard Davies

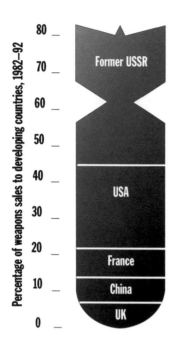

Percentage of weapons sales to developing countries, 1982–92

- 80 — Former USSR
- 70 —
- 60 —
- 50 —
- 40 — USA
- 30 —
- 20 — France
- 10 — China
- 0 — UK

Weapons sales to developing countries by the permanent members of the UN Security Council

Source: UNDP

Poverty is a common element to many conflicts. Another is the part played by governments of the industrialised nations through the international arms trade. In fact, over 80 per cent of that trade is carried out by the five Permanent Members of the UN Security Council. This trade adds further to the poverty which fuels conflict, by diverting the scarce resources of poor countries away from where they are most needed. Third World elites, who benefit in all sorts of ways from the trade, are only too happy to collude in, or even run, the process. Indeed, they often benefit doubly, since many weapons are purchased to repress civil dissent, and preserve an unjust status quo.

Church in Kibeho, Rwanda, where over 4000 Tutsis were murdered.

Photo: Robert Maletta

Time for a new vision

A shared world

Poverty affects us all, as individuals or nations. Denying huge numbers of people the chance to use their talents and realise their potential is an inefficient, wasteful way of running our world. And in the end we all suffer.

Despair and frustration are leading, at national and global levels, to social instability, violence, environmental damage, and massive increases in organised crime and drugs trafficking. Poor people and nations may bear the brunt, but we live in a shrinking, interdependent world. Affluent communities and nations cannot shelter indefinitely behind security systems and border controls.

Real security can never be built on poverty, even poverty apparently confined to another postcode or a distant continent. There is an urgent need for people in the rich world to join the millions of poor people who are working for a world where every human being enjoys his or her basic rights: there is no realistic alternative.

In fact, the idea of an end to the poverty which currently blights the lives of so many people begins more and more to seem not only realistic and realisable, but also the only hope for world survival.

The world's governments currently spend at least $800bn a year on their military requirements: reducing their expenditure by a little more than half a per cent would free enough money to finance basic education for all the world's children. Indeed, how can anyone claim that the world is too strapped for cash, when each day $1 trillion moves through the global financial markets?

Struggling for rights

Many of the world's poorest people have shown a vision lacked by most, if not all, governments. They are not content to be told that their rights are unattainable, that it is unrealistic to want clean water or enough to eat. They are demanding, half a century after the UN outlined its vision, that words be turned into actions. And they are beginning with their own situations, putting time and energy into transforming their own communities.

It's taken Janki Manjhi eight years to obtain proof that he owns the land that he and his family depend on for a living. Back in 1986 he moved on to government-owned land in the Indian state of Bihar. The government had allocated the land for distribution to landless farmers like Janki, but it was being illegally occupied by a landlord from a neighbouring town.

With help from Oxfam-funded Gram Nirman Kendra, the farmers campaigned for the eviction of the landlord and the right to claim the land for themselves. Eight years later — eight years of asking, and waiting, and promises that came to nothing — Janki holds the all-important piece of paper confirming that the land is his.

photo: Achinto

"This place was a mud hole when we first arrived, " says Maria Silva de Andrade. "We now have a school, a health post, water, and electricity." Maria and her husband live in Belém, at the mouth of the Amazon. Most of the city is below sea-level, and the swampy land where the poorest residents live is regularly flooded. When it rains the river branches rise, and the streets of the poorest shanty towns become ankle-deep in sewage and litter. Disease is a constant threat, and local community groups are doing what they can to improve health care there.

A municipal scheme to improve drainage and sanitation for half a million people will make for a safer environment, but Maria and 2,500 other people face losing their homes as a result. With help from the Oxfam-funded Belém Residents' Association, Maria and the other affected people are campaigning for compensation and better resettlement terms.

photo: Frances Rubin

Janki and Maria are driven by the urgency of their own needs, and also by a stubborn vision of their own rights as human beings: rights to a livelihood, and a safe, clean home. It is time for governments and international institutions to show as much vision as Janki and Maria, and

• re-affirm the basic rights (social and economic, as well as civil and political), of all human beings

• act to turn those rights into reality.

It is time, too, for ordinary people in the world's richer countries to add our voices to those of Janki and Maria, in demanding that they do so. Real change comes from the grassroots up.

Poster for Rural Workers Union, Brazil

photo: Jenny Matthews

Basic rights and an end to poverty

Only 200 years ago people still felt able to argue that keeping other human beings as slaves was perfectly compatible with leading a good, moral life. Abolitionists argued that human beings are born with an inalienable right to personal liberty; they demanded that this right should be enjoyed by all human beings, regardless of where they had been born or the colour of their skin. They succeeded in their struggle because ultimately people were forced to admit the justice of their cause; and also because slavery was seen to be an inefficient and wasteful system.

The years since the end of the Second World War have seen a further broadening in awareness of what being human means, or should mean. The Depression of the 1930s and the rise of fascism, in particular, showed the terrible consequences of denying the full humanity of others; the end of that war found many people consumed by longing for a world in which each individual would have their humanity recognised, and be able to live as full a life as possible. Systems which deny people this over-arching right, and the basic rights which safeguard it, were recognised as both morally wrong, and wasteful of human talent and potential. Such systems were seen, too, as a threat not just to the people they deprived, but to everyone. The conflagration of 1939-45 proved that, in the end, the consequences of denying certain people their basic rights are likely to engulf us all.

These experiences led to a concern to formalise basic rights, to get them agreed, written down, and, most importantly, recognised by the world's governments. The charters, covenants, and agreements listed below are some of the most important to have been drawn up, but similar moral convictions underpin many other documents, including a number of regional agreements like the African Charter on Human and People's Rights. Thus Oxfam's Global Basic Rights Charter draws on the definitions and perceptions which already form the basis for some of the most significant human rights instruments of the century.

International agreements on rights

- The United Nations Charter (1945): a treaty binding on all UN members, in other words, virtually all the world's states; concerned primarily with the maintenance of peace, but also includes the notion of the collective responsibility of all UN members for the promotion and safeguarding of human rights world-wide. Article 1 gives its aim as being "to achieve international co-operation in solving international problems of an economic, social, cultural or humanitarian character, and in promoting and encouraging respect for human rights and for fundamental freedoms for all without distinction as to race, sex, language, or religion."

The Charter brings all human beings within the scope of human rights – for too long, only privileged people were seen as having an automatic entitlement to human rights. It emphasises the concept of equality or non-discrimination. It implies that concern about human rights is not limited by national boundaries, but is a matter of legitimate international concern.

The UN Charter does not define human rights. This task was left to the UN itself and it was decided that an International Bill of Human Rights should be drawn up. This includes the following three instruments:

- The Universal Declaration of Human Rights (1948): enshrines the over-riding principle of non-discrimination, states that **all** people are entitled to the fulfilment of all human rights on an equal footing. (see page 107)

- International Covenant of Civil and Political Rights (1966)

- International Covenant of Economic, Social and Cultural Rights (1966)

All three confirm the notion already contained in the Charter that all persons are entitled to:
- civil and political rights, including the rights to life, integrity, liberty and security of the human person; administration of justice; privacy; freedom of religion or belief, and of opinion and expression; movement; assembly and association; political participation;
- economic, social, and cultural rights, including the rights to work; trade union membership and involvement; an adequate standard of living, including food, clothing, and housing; health care; education; participation in cultural life.

All persons are declared to be entitled to these rights without distinction of any kind, to be equal before the law, and entitled without any discrimination, to equal protection from the law.

- Geneva Conventions (1949): aim to limit violence and protect the fundamental rights of the individual in time of armed conflict.

- Convention on the Elimination of all forms of Racial Discrimination (1966): seeks to prevent and combat racist doctrines and practices, in order to promote understanding between races.

- International Convention on the Elimination of Discrimination against Women (1979): is an expression of the international community's determination to adopt measures required for the elimination of discrimination against women in all its forms and manifestations.

- Convention on the Rights of the Child (1989): sets out the rights of the child, and promotes the principle "in the best interests of the child".

- Rio Declaration on Environment and Development, and Agenda 21 (1992): commit governments to safeguarding the global environment. The Rio Declaration is a series of principles defining the rights and responsibilities of states; Agenda 21 offers a comprehensive and far-reaching programme for sustainable development at an international, national, and local level.

- Vienna Declaration and Programme of Action (1993): reaffirms the principle of universality, interdependence, and indivisibility of human rights; calls for concerted action to eradicate all forms of violence against women.

- Cairo Declaration (1994): (from the International Conference on Population and Development) seeks to affirm women's rights to reproductive health and control of their own fertility.

- Copenhagen Declaration and Programme of Action (1995): affirms the agreement of governments to take action aimed at promoting social justice, solidarity, and equality; defines poverty not simply as a lack of income resulting in hunger, ill health, homelessness, and limited access to education, but as being inextricably linked to a lack of control over resources, including land, skills, knowledge, capital, and social connections; states that the eradication of poverty "will require democratic participation and changes in economic structures to ensure access for all to resources".

(Many internationally agreed standards are not based on legally binding treaties, but there is an increasing reliance on declarations and statements of principles which not only represent important political commitments by governments, but also lay down the ground rules for international relations and the implementation of domestic policies.)

There have been attempts to depict some of these documents as utopian and unrealistic, to suggest that we cannot possibly hope to see *all* human beings realising their social and economic rights. Perhaps the best counter to such arguments is to look at what has been achieved in many parts of the world: the virtual eradication of cholera and other killer diseases by huge public sewage systems and comprehensive immunisation programmes, the introduction of universal free or nearly free education in so many countries, the resettlement and rehousing of all Europe's refugees after the Second World War.

Nor is it only rich countries which have achieved such miracles. Vietnam, a country crippled by decades of war, international isolation, and economic mismanagement, has literacy rates of over 90 per cent, and has managed to transform itself within a decade from a country gripped by near-famine to the world's third-largest rice exporter. Kerala is one of India's poorest states, but the state government has invested heavily in health care and education; as a result, infant mortality rates there are a quarter of the average for India, and virtually every Keralan child completes primary school. Mali, one of the world's poorest countries (155 out of 160 according to the UNDP), has transformed itself from a military dictatorship into a genuine democracy with a real commitment to protecting the rights of all its citizens, and to finding the mechanisms to resolve conflicts before they explode into violence.

Primary school in Ky Anh district, Vietnam.

photo: Sean Sprague

All these achievements, in both rich and poor areas, are vulnerable: all can be overturned. But they demonstrate clearly what can be achieved where there is a genuine will to tackle and solve even the most overwhelming problems.

Some commentators have tried to argue that civil and political rights are a luxury that poor nations cannot afford. They maintain that economic and social rights must take precedence, even if this means curtailing other rights. However, the "either/or" approach is misleading: there is, for example, plenty of evidence to suggest that an important factor in preventing famine from occurring when harvests fail is the existence of a free press.

The range of rights covered by international documents is a broad one, for no one right can exist in total isolation. Rights are interdependent, and realising one right makes it easier to realise others. The more years of education a woman has, the healthier she and her children are likely to be. When squatter settlers are able to exercise their democratic rights, they are more likely to obtain clean water and sanitation. A farmer with security of tenure is more likely to be able to send his or her children to school.

The following pages look at the ten rights listed in Oxfam's Global Basic Rights Charter. They set out in more detail the status of those rights in international law, and the consequences for ordinary people when they are denied, and they look at some of the ways in which people — individuals, community groups, organisations like Oxfam, local government workers, and national governments — are working to turn these rights from theoretical concepts into solid everyday reality.

The right to enough to eat

recognised:

- The International Covenant of Economic, Social and Cultural Rights recognises the right of everyone to an adequate standard of living and "the fundamental right of everyone to be free from hunger".
- Signatories to the Covenant on the Rights of the Child have pledged themselves to combating malnutrition among children.
- The Geneva Conventions prohibit the use of starvation as an instrument of war, including in this the destruction of resources such as livestock and crops.

denied:

- 800 million people in the world are severely malnourished or starving.
- In Bangladesh malnutrition rates are three times higher among girls than among boys.

Even in a year of good rains, most families in Bweri, a village on the shores of Lake Victoria in north-west Tanzania, can grow food to last only three to five months each year. For the rest of the year they have to depend on casual labour on building sites, or petty trade in maize flour, fish, firewood, and charcoal.

A survey in 1992 showed that 38 per cent of all families were eating only one meal a day. About 6 per cent of all children were malnourished. The price of maize had doubled over the previous year, and many families were trying to survive on cassava, which is low in protein.

Ironically, Bweri is actually a major protein-exporter. Every month, over 80 tonnes of frozen Nile Perch fillets are processed in the new Fishpak factory, for export to Holland, Spain, Germany, and the UK. Fishpak brings employment to Bweri, and hard currency to Tanzania, but the fish is being harvested and removed from a community already chronically deficient in protein.

The growth of the export business has increased local fish prices. In the 18 months after Fishpak started operating in Bweri, prices had increased six-fold. "We can buy the skeletons from Fishpak, for making soup," explains Bibie Usufu, "but we don't eat much fish now because it's scarce. The price is too high. All the fishermen sell to Fishpak. Prices have risen so much that fish has become almost unaffordable to local people."

The Fishpak factory.
photo: Geoff Sayer

- Large commercial Zimbabwean farmers, owners of the country's most fertile land, leave 40 per cent of that land uncultivated; one third of all children in Zimbabwe have symptoms of chronic malnutrition.
- Economic reforms in Peru in 1991 saw food prices rise by 2,500 per cent in one year, and the number of people living in extreme poverty double.

but possible:

"We've grown sorghum here since 1985," says Arakudi Apalla Lobe, of Kenya's drought-prone Turkana region. "We joined a training course on *bund* construction, and had a good harvest in that first year, just like this year's. The yield varies, but we've had a harvest every year — it's never failed, even during the drought years."

Arakudi has worked with the Lokitaung Pastoral Development Project to improve her small *shamba*, or sorghum patch. Her environment is a harsh one, many people would say an impossible one. But Arakudi has proved that even in the harshest of environments hunger does not have to be inevitable.

"Building the *bunds* was hard, but we've proved it's worthwhile. We all worked together, all the project members, for five weeks to raise the *bunds* for this *shamba*. We moved from *shamba* to *shamba* until they were all completed.

"Now we work with two other families who have *shambas* nearby. Because we're close to the harvest they're helping us now to keep birds off the sorghum. This year we'll harvest six to eight bags, in about ten days' time. Until then I stay here all day with my daughter, Napocho, to frighten off the birds, and my husband comes to spend the night, to guard the crop against thieves.

"We'll keep some of the sorghum to eat, but most we'll sell, so that we can buy another five goats, and pay off the credit we've taken from the project store. We lost 25 goats during the drought, and have 15 left, with their kids. Ten are in milk, and now

photo: Geoff Sayer

the rains have come we hope things will get better."

In such a precarious existence, running up a small debt can be the prelude to disaster. The Lokitaung project store keeps prices low, and gives its members credit through difficult times. "It's been a big help," explains Arakudi. "Just last week I bought sugar on credit. We have to eat when we're to do the hard work of cultivating the *shamba*. The store has helped us through every year; the credit has been especially valuable during the hard years, like 1992."

The right to clean water

recognised:

- The International Covenant of Civil and Political Rights recognises the right to life, and requires governments to take measures to eliminate malnutrition and epidemics, in order to reduce infant mortality and increase life expectancy. The International Covenant of Economic, Social and Cultural Rights recognises the right to the highest attainable standard of physical and mental health. With approximately 80 per cent of diseases and over one-third of all deaths in the developing world caused by contaminated water, clearly the right to clean water is an essential component of these rights.
- The UN Conference on the Environment and Development (1992) recognises the obligation of individual states to safeguard minimum standards of water purity.
- The Geneva Conventions oblige warring parties to protect the natural environment, and prohibit the use of methods of warfare which are intended to contaminate water sources.
- The Rio Declaration and Agenda 21 recognise the vital importance of safe water supplies and environmentally-sensitive sanitation for protecting the environment, improving health, and alleviating poverty.

denied:

- More than 1 billion people have no clean water or sanitation.
- 25,000 people — the equivalent of the population of Durham — die each day from water-borne disease.
- In Zambia over 22 per cent of the people in rural areas have to walk more than 1km to reach their nearest water source.
- In Lima, Peru, poor people pay up to $3 for a cubic metre of contaminated water from a private vendor: middle-class households pay $0.5 for the same amount of clean tap water.

In poor communities throughout the world it is women who bear the burden of collecting the day's water for their families. Many have to spend hours of every day walking to sources several miles away. Spinal problems and severe headaches are a common result of carrying containers of water weighing up to 22kg (40lb). What is more, sickness and death may be carried home, along with the water. Untreated water, possibly from a muddy water-hole shared with cattle, can be lethal, especially for young children.

Photo: John Ogle

but possible:

"Before we had to get water from a pool 2km away. The water was dirty and lots of us got ill. Now the health of the people here is better."

Oun Svey is head of Prey Veng village, in Thmar Puok, close to Cambodia's border with Thailand. Despite nominal government control, this is still Khmer Rouge country, and Thmar Puok is an area torn by violence and conflict. Armed bandits, warlords, and smugglers hold sway here as well.

And it is an area of great poverty, where water is a particular problem. "Either we have bad flooding," says Ros Monichot, Programme Supervisor for the Oxfam-funded Khmer Buddhist Association, "or near drought conditions. Because of this we have developed traditional ways of locating water sources.

"Termites show where there is water. If you see a small hill, that slowly gets bigger and bigger, this indicates that termites are there, a sure indication that there is water there too.

"Or find a tree. A hard variety, that we usually use for building houses. Look at its roots. Find out which way the roots are growing. Water will also be in that direction.

"We can also fish for water. We attach a cotton wool ball to a piece of string on a stick and search for water under the ground. You can tell the difference between shaking in the wind and the shaking which means that water is present.

"But it's not enough just to find water. You then have to dig 30 to 40 centimetres down, put a lid over the top. If moisture rises up, you know there is definitely water there. After this you start digging a three-metre hole. If it is humid at three metres, you then dig down another ten metres. Here there will be good water."

War keeps people poor in Thmar Puok. It prevents them from putting down firm roots and investing time and energy in finding long-term solutions to their problems. But even against such a bleak background, the Khmer Buddhist Association has been able to help people to claim their basic right to clean water. Prey Veng is one of ten villages where it has provided training and materials to enable villagers to locate water and then sink their own wells.

The well-digging has had other results. It has got people working together in a situation where trust does not come easily: "they have changed their way of looking at things," says Ros Monichot, "and they are now working together in the Buddhist way." And it has given women a new status and a new vision of what they can achieve: "Everything in society is decided by men," comments Ros Monichot, "and women are not asked. The wells project has changed things. More women are joining us than men. In Prey Veng six wells were dug by women."

photo: Nic Dunlop

The right to a livelihood

recognised:

- The International Covenant on Economic, Social and Cultural Rights recognises the right to work.
- It also recognises the right to just and fair conditions of work, including the rights to work in safe and healthy conditions and to form and join a trade union.
- The International Covenant of Civil and Political Rights recognises the right not to be subjected to slavery or forced labour.
- The Convention on the Elimination of Discrimination against Women and the Convention on the Elimination of all Forms of Racial Discrimination articulate the right not to be discriminated against on the grounds of gender or race in the realm of work.
- The 1995 Social Summit Declaration commits states planning development schemes, such as large dams, not to damage the livelihoods of those living in the area. It also commits governments to producing national poverty-eradication plans by 1996, and to drawing these plans up with the participation of people living in poverty.

denied:

- One in four of the world's people live in profound poverty, unable to meet their basic needs.
- Conservative estimates put the number of child prostitutes in Thailand, Sri Lanka, and the Philippines at 500,000.
- Six million black Zimbabwean subsistence farmers depend for a living on 20 per cent of the land; the best 20 per cent is owned by 4,500, mostly white, commercial farmers; on average, commercial farms are 800 times larger than subsistence farms.
- In real terms, average wages in Zambia in 1991 were a quarter of their mid-1970s' level.
- In Britain around one-third of workers now earn less than 68 per cent of the national average wage, a 25 per cent increase since 1979.

In 1993 the privatisation of Zambia's maize marketing system, and a failure of private sector traders to fill the vacuum left by the state system, left women farmers in Eastern Province with bumper crops — and no way of selling them. Farmers in Chipata district are about 45km from the nearest maize marketing centre. Since there is no bus service, the only means of reaching it is on foot, and the women cannot afford the lost labour time. Forced to sell their crops to a single local buyer, many eventually had to accept prices 25 per cent below what the crops were really worth. Many had to barter their crops for necessities — one woman sold a 15kg tin of maize for just two bars of soap, a quarter the value of the maize at the previous year's prices.

LOS PLAGUICIDAS SON VENENOSOS

Oxfam-funded education campaign with seasonal agricultural workers.

Julio Etchart

"We are paid to work ten hours," says Luisa Pina, a labourer in Chile's Central Valley, "but during the harvest we work for at least 14 hours with no extra pay. Last year I became sick. It was after we were spraying Temick [a severely toxic pesticide] on the peas. I was told I would not be paid if I could not work, so I continued working. Many other women suffered from stomach complaints. But we all continued working ... we cannot live if we do not have work."

Unemployment

	% Unemployed	% Population in rural areas
Nicaragua	14	39
Sudan	13	76.8
Sri Lanka	14.1	78.6
USA	10.1	24.4

Source: *World Economic and Social Survey 1994*

The figures above are misleading: unemployment, as it is understood in industrialised countries, is a modern, largely urban phenomenon. It is a concept which cannot always easily be applied to the situation in developing countries, particularly ones which are predominantly rural.

It may be relevant for the few countries where the land is farmed by large commercial operations, employing a work-force in much the same way as a factory might. In traditional agriculture, however, characterised by family units cultivating small plots, low productivity may be endemic, but unemployment is an unknown concept. Often marginal traditional farmers may have to spend at least part of the year as paid labourers, possibly on a larger farm, because the small family plot is not large enough for subsistence.

Fluid and informal systems like these make calculating employment rates almost impossible, particularly given the very complex working roles played by most women. In most African countries, for example, two-thirds or more of the population is still rural, and wage-earners are only a small proportion of the total labour force. In such a situation, official rural unemployment rates, and therefore unemployment rates for the whole country, are very low. This can give a completely misleading idea of the incidence of poverty in a given country, and can also mask very high rates of urban unemployment.

but possible:

"We have a problem here, mostly economic, about how to send our children to school, and cope with daily life," says Ibu Rambu Otu, of the small Indonesian island of Sumba. "We had heard good things about Wahana from other groups, and thought they might be able to help."

Wahana, a local community organisation, began by organising workshops to discuss all the problems facing women in West Sumba, such as the shortage of drinking water, poor health, and their heavy workload.

At the heart of all these problems, the women recognised, was a lack of income. Wahana has helped the women in Ibu Otu's village to buy goats and rice seed, and to set up a village savings and credit scheme.

People there face regular "hungry times", because they finish the grain they have harvested several months before the next harvest is due. With Wahana's guidance the women have set up vegetable gardens to tide them over those months. They now have fresh produce to eat and sell, though they are nervous about taking their produce to market. "We're not sure if the vegetables will sell, and we're afraid about making the journey," explained the group's Treasurer, Korlina Kahilep. However, supported by Wahana and the other members of the women's group in their village, the women will shortly be trying out new markets for their produce.

photo: Imam Hartoyo

The right to a home

recognised

- The International Covenant on Economic, Social and Cultural Rights recognises the right to adequate housing.
- Many other international agreements recognise the same right — which is seen as more than a right to a roof over one's head. Most agreements define it as a right to live somewhere in peace, security, and dignity. Most define adequate housing as:
  - having legal security of tenure
  - being affordable
  - providing sufficient space
  - providing adequate protection from cold, damp, heat or rain
  - allowing access to employment, health and education services, and social facilities
  - being appropriate to the culture of those living there.

denied:

- There are reckoned to be 11 million homeless people in the world.
- In the developing countries overall, as many as one person in three is homeless or in severely substandard housing.
- A third of the population in most Third World cities are squatters; at least 600 million people are living there in conditions which threaten their health and even lives.
- 37 million people have been driven from their homes by violence and armed conflict; over 80 per cent of them are women and children.
- If current trends continue, there will be more than 100 million refugees by 2000.
- One in every hundred Africans (over four million people) is a refugee.
- Between 1960 and 1982 an estimated 3.5 million black South Africans were forcibly moved from their homes: it will be many years before the new South Africa can hope to deal with the housing crisis which has resulted.

Poverty goes to town

Some 2,300 million people, 43 per cent of the world's population, now lives in urban areas. In the developing world the urban population is rising by about 50 million each year. Currently about a third of all town dwellers in the Third World are squatters. In most cities, the housing supply and the demand for labour are unable to keep pace with the expansion of the urban population, so by the end of the century shanty-town dwellers are likely to make up half the total urban population in most developing countries.

Living space in the squatter settlements is usually cramped and insecure. Basic privacy, let alone a quiet space where children might do their homework, are unknown luxuries. Proper ventilation, adequate lighting, clean water supplies, and sanitation become particularly essential in the overcrowded conditions of the shanty towns; but they are likely to be non-existent. Though the casual work most people depend on provides incomes below the poverty line, much of their pay may go on travelling from peripheral squatter settlements to wherever they can find that work. In many areas, high crime rates are one indication that people have lost the security of old family and community ties.

In developing countries, the urban population is growing at a rate of at least 3.6 per cent each year. We are seeing a new trend: not just to an increasingly urbanised world, but to an urbanisation of poverty.

Port-au-Prince shanty town, Haiti.

photo: Jenny Matthews

but possible:

"It's very good to see the people coming back to Roosboom," says Mavis Sisane. "They were sent away unjustly, and now they have come back to their own land."

In 1976, under South Africa's apartheid laws, most of Mavis's neighbours were forced to leave their homes and land, and dumped in a distant township. For the next 15 years the exiled community continued to fight to be allowed to return to Roosboom, to the land they legally owned, and which had been in their families for generations. They lobbied the government, and put forward their case at public hearings. In 1990 some of them reoccupied their land, and started to rebuild their community. Finally, the whole community was given permission to return.

Throughout their struggle the Association for Rural Advancement (AFRA) helped them document their claim to their land, provided them with training, and publicised their case nationally.

Going home to Roosboom was the end of a struggle and the beginning of new challenges. Now that people have returned to their ancestral land, AFRA is helping them to develop it, to establish a communal farm, and build new homes, a new school and a new community.

Angel Nkosi was born and brought up during her community's exile in the township, and had never known rural life, but is happy to have returned to her ancestral land. "I like this place," she says. "If it's nice weather you can sleep with the doors and windows open. In the township I was scared to do this. I want to stay here in Roosboom, because it is the land of our great-great-grandmothers. They bought it a long time ago."

Agnes Sokhulu, aged 75, returned to Roosboom in 1990.

photo: Cedric Nunn

The right to an education

recognised:

- The International Covenant on Education, Social, and Cultural Rights obliges states to provide compulsory and free primary education for all.
- The Convention on the Rights of the Child states further that individuals should be able to choose where they are educated and what sort of education they receive; and all states should take measures to eliminate indoctrination from the curriculum, and make sure that the education they provide meets the needs of minority groups.

denied:

- Nearly one in three people in the Third World has not learnt to read or write.
- Worldwide, in 1991 over 125 million children, between the ages of six and eleven, were not enrolled in school; at least two-thirds were girls.
- El Salvador publishes 1 book for every 1,000,000 of its inhabitants; Spain publishes 714.

Wangoi is ten; her brother Mwangi is fourteen. When Mwangi was in Standard Three at school, their father died. The small farm where they had grown up was not enough to support the family without the extra income that their father had brought in from labouring on other, larger, farms. Their mother had to leave, and took the family to Nairobi. Now they live in Kibera, an area of poor housing on the edge of the city.

"I don't go to school," says Mwangi, "because Mother can't afford it. We don't like Nairobi. We want to go back to our village, and go to school again. Mother says she will take us back when she has enough money, when she has saved enough. Most days I walk into town with my mother — she sells peanuts in the park. We beg there. Sometimes we get 20 shillings [35p] to take home."

photo: Geoff Sayer

Average for selected developed countries
182 books

Average for selected developing countries
1 book

Access to information: published books per 200,000 inhabitants in rich and poor countries
Source: UNESCO

but possible:

"We had been broadcasting for a few months," says Bourkary Tamboura, a presenter with Radio Daande Douentza (The Voice of Douentza), "when we decided to find out what people thought about the impact of the station. It came out that some women were so impressed by what we were broadcasting that they were fattening cattle especially to sell to buy a radio in order to follow our programmes." In fact, in the six months following the first broadcast of Douentza's only local radio station, the number of radios owned there leapt by 140 per cent.

The 168,000 people living in the Douentza region of eastern Mali are poor and mostly illiterate. Many years of low rainfall have contributed to increasing desertification, and farmers and herders now compete for land and water resources.

People here have little access to information, and health and education services are few and far between. There are no telephones, no newspapers, no postal services. Before Radio Daande Douentza went out on the air, the only radio programmes people could pick up were in languages which no one could understand.

In June 1992, the Near East Foundation, a local community organisation, took part in a training seminar on environmental degradation, and how to inform and educate people about the issue. One suggestion they came back with was to start their own radio station, broadcasting initially in Fulani, the language of commerce in Fouentza, and understood by 85 per cent of the population.

The station was an immediate success, partly because it was providing information not hitherto easily available to people, but also because for the first time the people of the region felt that they had gained a voice. Before long it had expanded its service to its current eight hours a day, seven days a week, mostly going out in the evening, when people have the time to listen. Opinion polls indicate that 86 per cent of its possible audience regularly listens to the station, which puts its annual running costs at just 25p per listener per year.

They are not passive listeners: 80 per cent claim to have responded in some way to what they have heard, to have changed the way they do things, or the way they think. Demand for literacy classes more than doubled in the station's first year, as has the number of children being brought for immunisation. A recent survey discovered that people in Fouentza are far better informed about the causes and prevention of AIDS than people in any other region of Mali: most people interviewed claimed to have got this information from the radio and, in particular, from a series of seven programmes dealing specifically with the subject.

"People here are mainly involved in agriculture and cattle-breeding," says Yacouba Demme, of the Near East Foundation. "So there is a need for good technical advice. Also there are a lot of health problems, so advice on how to prevent or treat certain diseases is also required. There are almost no health services in the area, so many people live nowhere near a dispensary.

"In addition to these material needs, people have other needs which are just as important, such as information, civics education, and democratisation training. We avoid taking sides; we don't give support to any particular political party; we don't allow them air-time to voice their political ideas, except at election time, when we invite them all to come on air to present their manifestos.

"The rest of our programmes deal with technical and legal matters. For example, the Constitution says that it is illegal to lock someone up for more than 48 hours without charge. If people are not aware of these rights, they may fall victim to corrupt local officials or even simple administrative mistakes."

Radio Daande Douentza goes on air.

photo: James Hawkins

Average for selected developed countries
77 years

Average for selected developing countries
43 years

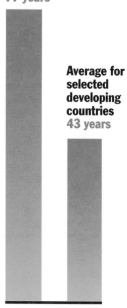

Life expectancy at birth in rich and poor countries

Source: *World Guide 1995*

The right to health care

recognised:

- The International Covenant on Social, Economic and Cultural rights recognises the right to the highest attainable standard of physical and mental health. States are committed, not just to providing curative health care, but also to avoiding measures which might damage people's health.

denied:

- Ten per cent of children in the Third World die before their fifth birthday.
- Every fortnight more children die from preventable diseases than were killed in the genocide in Rwanda.
- Half of all women in Africa and south Asia, and two-thirds of all pregnant women in both regions, are anaemic.
- In India, more women die from pregnancy and birth-related causes in one week, than in Europe in one year.
- One billion people never see a health professional.
- According to UNICEF, half the amount spent annually on cigarettes in Europe would save the lives of all the children who die from preventable diseases.
- Reproductive health services, including family planning, are available to only half of all women in south Asia, and one in ten women in sub-Saharan Africa.

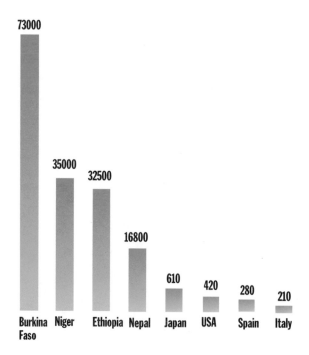

Inhabitants per physician

Source: *World Development Report 1995*

Uganda is one of the world's most severely indebted countries. In 1994, the country was scheduled to pay $162 million in debt service payments, which represents over four-fifths of the country's export earnings. This compares with the $120 million which the government spends on health and education combined. More than one baby in ten there dies before it reaches its first birthday. Among children under five, the main killers are malaria, diarrhoea, pneumonia, and malnutrition. All these illnesses could be prevented or cured with basic health care and adequate sanitation.

Women, too, are dying from lack of basic health care. When Enid Tusiime developed complications during labour, her mother-in-law, Geraldine Kagija, hesitated to send her into hospital. She knew that there would be fees to pay, and she had no money. Geraldine's land grows enough food for the family, but there is barely enough cash to buy salt and soap. Hospital fees were more or less out of the question.

After two days of labour, Enid did go into the hospital in Mbarara district. She reached it after a two-hour journey on a home-made stretcher carried by her family, but it was too late. Her child died and, after a month in intensive care, so did she.

Her family was left with a debt to the hospital of £55, which they have struggled to repay by selling one of their two cows, and working on the hospital's land in lieu of payment. The hospital would prefer cash, but the family has none.

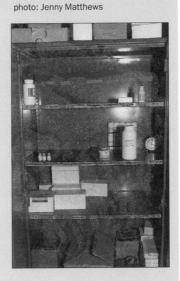

This clinic dispensary near Mbale is virtually empty.

photo: Jenny Matthews

but possible:

"There's been a great change in Bowerbank," says Angela Cooke. "When I started there was a low percentage of kids, maybe a quarter, who were immunised. I asked the Ministry nurse to come in, and now 95 per cent are OK."

Bowerbank, in downtown Kingston, Jamaica, has a bad reputation. Violence and drugs are a major problem, and leaving school with a Bowerbank address does little for a youngster's job prospects. Half of Bowerbank is jobless, and the lure of the corner gangs is seductive for young people looking for excitement, money, and a way out of the ghetto.

But Bowerbank is changing. Jamaica has a long tradition of community organisation, led by women, which has its roots in the slave plantations of the eighteenth and nineteenth centuries. Then, women came together for mutual support while the men worked in the fields. Now, Jamaica has one of the highest levels of female-headed households in the world, and the spirit of co-operation and action is still strong.

The women of Bowerbank got tired of the rubbish in their streets, the poor sanitation, and the lack of decent schools and health care. In 1989, with help from Oxfam, UNICEF, and the Jamaican Ministry of Health, they began to do something about it, starting with their children's health.

photo: John Barraclough

Angela Cooke was one of the first people to be trained to help the community get informed about their right to social security and other welfare payments. Today she works on community health and is responsible for immunisation and nutrition clinics.

The Ministry and UNICEF pay for the regular clinic, and children get a free "I've been fully immunised" T-shirt when they've had all their jabs. "There has also been a noticeable weight gain among the children, who are now average for their height," says Angela.

Between making house-to-house visits and chivvying mothers who have not had their children immunised, Angela offers nutrition training and gives out condoms. But there's more to the welfare of the community than clinics and contraception. Not short of confidence, the group are tackling their next problem: re-location.

The barrack-style houses of Bowerbank were always intended to be temporary, but most teenagers have lived most of their lives there. The city council has plans to move the residents to what they say is a better site on the outskirts of Kingston. The women are not convinced. They are using their new organisational and negotiating skills to make sure the new site is better than Bowerbank, and they have vowed to move only on their own terms.

The right to a safe environment

recognised:

• The Rio Declaration, and Agenda 21, declare that states have an obligation to protect the environment, not just for those alive today, but also for future generations, and that they should take pre-emptive action to avert any "serious or irreversible" damage to the environment.

denied:

- 25 billion tonnes of soil in Asia are currently being lost to erosion each year.
- A further 21 million hectares of land turns to barren desert each year.
- Each year 17-18 million hectares of forest and woodland are destroyed.
- Cattle ranchers in Latin America are burning the rain-forest at a rate of 2.5 million hectares a year.
- Many fish stocks in the industrialised world — including Atlantic cod and herring — have all but died out. To make up for this loss, catches are being increased off areas such as the west coast of Africa.

During the 1980s the consumption of shrimps doubled in the USA and Japan, leading to a huge increase in exports from south-east Asia. Shellfish farming is now one of the largest sources of foreign exchange for poor countries like Bangladesh and Vietnam. As a result, mangrove forests along the coasts of many tropical countries have been decimated, with disastrous consequences.

In the Philippines, mangrove swamps have been cleared at an average rate of 3,000 hectares a year to make way for large commercial prawn farms, most of them owned by Japanese companies producing for export to Japan. These swamps now cover less than one-tenth of their original area. The destruction of the mangrove fish-breeding grounds means a progressive lowering of fish catches each year for local fishing communities. On current trends the Philippines' remaining mangrove swamps will be destroyed within a decade.

In Bangladesh the expansion of shrimp farming has been associated with the forcible eviction of small-holder farmers, often involving considerable violence. In addition, the demands of the shrimp industry for fresh water has severely depressed the water table in many areas, creating water shortages and adding to existing problems of salinity.

Fishermen bringing in their early morning catch, northern Luzon, Philippines.
photo: Tricia Spanner

but possible:

"Before the dykes were repaired," says a woman from Vietnam's Ky Anh district, "we would often have to escape to safety through floodwater up to our necks, carrying our children on our heads."

"Before the dykes were repaired," says Mr Lanh, Secretary of the Ky Anh Education Committee, "schools were damaged each year. Ky Tho school, for example, was flooded seven times. Children missed a lot of schooling. Classes had to be held in people's houses." When, that is, a house could be found that the floods had spared.

Ky Anh district is one of Vietnam's poorest: drought-prone during the dry season, but subject to huge seawater floods when typhoons sweep in off the South China Sea. Over 200 years people there gradually developed a 40-mile system of protective embankments, but in the late 1980s the system had fallen into disrepair. Many stretches had been bombed during the war with the USA. In the decade of desperate poverty which followed the war, people lacked the resources to repair and maintain the dykes, and they degenerated still further.

Without their protection, each year brought similar tragedies during the typhoon season: homes, schools, and clinics wrecked, crops destroyed, the soil left salt-soaked and useless. "From my office," says Mr Tran, Chair of the Ky Anh People's Committee, "you would just have seen miles and miles of empty land, no one on the roads. Everywhere round here was barren. People looked weak and sad; they had no energy. They survived on edible roots for many months each year." The men left, to search for work abroad or in the south of the country: in 1990 Ky Tho village saw half its able-bodied men forced to leave.

When Oxfam mounted an emergency food programme in the district during the late 1980s, people were very clear about their longer-term needs: help with repairing the dykes. With the aid of an Oxfam food-for-work programme, they have now repaired nearly half the dyke system.

It has been an enormous community effort — one stretch alone took 380,000 person-hours to rebuild; there were often 5,000 local people working there. Cranes and heavy machinery are unavailable here, so tons of earth and rocks were transported by hand. Women planted 1.2 million mangrove tree seedlings on the sea-ward side of the dykes to protect them from wave damage.

Today life has returned to Ky Anh. Rice yields are already up by 15 per cent (it will take another five years to wash the salt from the soil), and the irrigated area has doubled in size. The dykes have also made it possible once more to supplement incomes by rearing shrimp in specially constructed lagoons on the landward side, and to make salt. Most of the men are now back at least part of the year, the decades of disrupted schooling are over. Among the people of Ky Anh there is a new sense of optimism and confidence in the future.

Repairing the dykes.

photo: Keith Bernstein

The right to protection from violence

recognised:

- The International Covenant of Civil and Political Rights guarantees the right to liberty and security, to life and to freedom from torture, or cruel, inhumane or degrading punishments.
- The Geneva Conventions forbid attacks or threats of violence against civilian populations, and rape.
- The Geneva Conventions prohibit ethnically-based massacres.
- The Inhumane Weapons Convention and Landmines Protocol governs the indiscriminate use of anti-personnel mines.
- The Declaration on the Elimination of Violence against Women, adopted by the UN General Assembly in 1994, condemns violence against women.

denied:

- There are currently 82 recognised large-scale conflicts going on in the world.
- In 1994 up to a million people were murdered in Rwanda in the space of a month.
- In the USA a woman is badly beaten every 18 minutes.
- China's One-Child Policy is estimated to have resulted in the deaths of more than one million first-born baby girls.
- 2,000 men, women, and children are killed, blinded, or dismembered by landmines every month; there are about 100,000,000 scattered unexploded around the world. They can cost as little as $3, but dismantling each one costs up to $1,000.

Number of wars

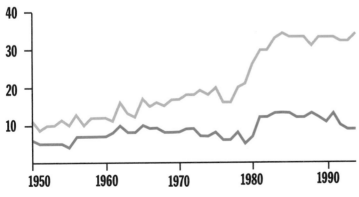

Armed conflicts with more than 1000 deaths
Armed conflicts with more than 100,000 deaths

Wars since 1950
Source: Worldwatch

- The annual cost of the UN's whole emergency, peacekeeping and humanitarian operations is about the same as it costs to run the New York City Fire Department.
- Most of the victims of Angola's civil war were children; nearly 20 years of fighting have left the country so poor that one baby in three dies before its first birthday, usually from malnutrition, malaria, or measles.

Laying crosses on the steps of St Martin-in-the-Fields, London, on the first anniversary of the massacres in Rwanda

photo: Jenny Matthews

"We were attacked by cattle raiders working for the government," remembers Amer Kuay, a 29-year-old Dinka woman from Sudan's Upper Nile District. "They took all our cattle. They burned our houses. They took all our belongings. We were left with no tools and hardly any seed, so we harvested very little. By February we started to starve.

"There were still attacks by Nuer raiders. So we decided to cross the Nile to Yirol District, where it was safer. We had to wait in the marshes for some time to get a fishing boat to take us across. We had no money to pay, so I had to give my daughters' clothes to the fisherman.

"Some of the people in our group were dying of hunger even as we started to walk from our village. Young children and old people died. I lost my youngest girl. She was just two years old."

At least a million people have died in Sudan, and another 1.5 million have been driven from their homes into camps, across borders or into the bush. Long-standing tribal rivalries and disputes over cattle and grazing grounds, previously contained by traditional mechanisms for resolving conflicts, are being integrated into a wider conflict, Sudan's long-running civil war between north and south; and they are being settled by automatic weapons. Such atrocities are not new. What is new is the destructive capacity of all sides in the conflict, and their willingness to use that capacity ruthlessly.

but possible:

There are two mosques in the small Pakistani village of Goth Janano, one for Sunnis and one for Shias. Six Hindu families also live in the village. There is considerable potential for religious tensions, but local community leaders are dedicated to resolving any conflicts, and keeping communication open between people of different sects and faiths.

"In the last days of Muharram there's a lot of grief and sorrow," says Muhammad Ruksh, one of the village leaders. "This is when we relive the death of the grandson of the Prophet. During this time, we have a session of mourning every evening. At this time even the Hindus join us, which helps to bind the community together.

"I want to share a fear of mine with you: every Friday, outside speakers from the Shia and Sunni sects come to the village and talk at the mosques. I have encouraged a Shia and a Sunni to get elected on to our village committee, so that they have to work together and achieve positive things. I've organised other committees so that both sects have to work together, one on health, one on registering births and deaths, and so on. If we can't stop it [i.e. the divisions being created by outsiders] getting out of hand, things will get into a real mess. We're working to stem the tide.

A young girl studying the Koran.
photo: Maryam Iqbal

"We are having a series of lectures in the village at the moment about human development: when people started living in communities, building houses, and so on. We would like some support from Oxfam, to help people understand that assistance isn't just about projects, but can be about opening your mind. That, I think, is just as important."

The right to equality of opportunity

recognised:

- The right to equality of opportunity is intrinsic to all other basic rights, and accepted as a basic norm.
- It is also specifically recognised by, among other documents, the International Covenant on Cultural and Political Rights, the International Covenant on Economic, Social and Cultural Rights, the International Convention on the Elimination of all

Discrimination against Women, the Convention on the Elimination of All Forms of Racial Discrimination, and the Universal Declaration of Human Rights.

denied:

- Worldwide, women are paid on average 30-40 per cent less than men for the same jobs.
- One person in ten worldwide is disabled: in most countries they have fewer education and employment opportunities than other people in their society.
- Literacy rates in Vietnam are well over 90 per cent for the majority Kinh ethnic group; among the ethnic minority groups of the country's mountainous regions, the rate is more like 12 per cent.
- Spending on health for Israeli citizens is $350; for Palestinians in the Occupied Territories it is $35. Infant mortality rates are five times higher in the Occupied Territories than in Israel.

"I finished Primary Seven at the end of 1991," says Faith Muhindo Tembao, a cleaner at Uganda's Kagando Hospital. "I wanted to go to Bwera Secondary School — it was very important for me, but we didn't have enough money for the fees. My brother William was in Secondary Two at Bwera; now he's in Secondary Four and he'll want to continue to Secondary Six.

"Boys take most of the places in secondary school. Some girls don't have the money to go, some just don't want to go. At 14 and 15 and 16 they start thinking of marriage, but not me. I won't get married early. My parents had no schooling and they regret it.

"I've managed to save 20,000 shillings; my mother looks after it for me. It's to help my brother if he wants to continue after Secondary Four. Or I may need to help the others with primary school fees. I'd like to be at school myself, but I don't mind if I can't go. Without my help even the younger ones might have to stop. When William has a job he should be able to help. It is more difficult for girls ... more difficult to do what they want."

photo: Geoff Sayer

photo: Emma Gough

but possible:

Conservative estimates put the proportion of disabled people in El Salvador at 10 per cent. Given the country's recent bitter civil war, that is almost certainly an under-estimate. They receive little assistance from the state, just the most basic of primary health care. Many disabled people receive no formal education at all, let alone any which recognises their particular needs. Their chances of finding a means of livelihood are slim.

Most of the 11 disabled people in the ceramics workshop run by ACOGIPRI are deaf. They have never attended school, never been taught to read or write, never even learnt to use sign language. As a result, most have lived for years locked in their own private world, unable to make themselves understood or understand the people round them. For most of their lives, they have been regarded as "unemployable".

The training provided by ACOGIPRI in ceramic production has given them the oppor-tunity to discover abilities no-one ever believed they possessed, and learn a whole range of new skills. Working with furnaces that reach up to 1060°C, they produce beautiful, original ceramic pottery and moulded stoneware, now selling well to the El Salvadorean middle classes. ACOGIPRI helps with administration and marketing, but all production is organised by the workers. Manuel Orillana, the production manager, is deaf himself.

After a special eight-month training from a Japanese designer, they branched confid-ently out into new styles, which made it possible for them to start thinking about reaching new markets. They now travel abroad to sell their wares at craft markets, and have established outlets in Guatemala and Honduras. In 1994 they hit the UK market, through the Oxfam mail-order catalogue.

ACOGIPRI, most of whose members are disabled themselves, tries to provide some of the opportunities which disabled people are denied by the society in which they live. As well as running the ceramics workshop, it provides courses in social skills, literacy, computer skills, marketing, and manage-ment, and special leadership training pro-grammes for disabled women. It keeps up a constant campaign to have public buildings and areas made accessible to disabled people, and to overcome all the other obstacles which prevent them from playing a full part in the life of El Salvador.

The right to a say in their future

recognised:

- The International Covenant on Cultural and Political Rights recognises the right to a vote and to take part in public affairs, to freedom of assembly and freedom of expression.

denied:

- Only 48 per cent of the world's people live in multi-party democracies. Over 400 million (8 per cent of total population) live in countries under military rule.
- In 1993 there were only six female heads of government in the world.
- At the UN only six of the 184 member countries have a female permanent representative.
- Developing countries account for more than three-quarters of the IMF's membership, but they have only one-third of the voting share.
- Since 1967 Israeli authorities and settlers have confiscated over two-thirds of the land area in the West Bank, and 40 per cent of the land in the Gaza Strip, leaving Palestinians with little control over land, water sources, or employment opportunities.

Sabitri Devi thinks for a minute. It has been a long time since anyone asked her how old she is. She thinks she's 40, but when people around her laugh, she revises this upwards: 45. Eight children.

Not so long ago, people like Sabitri would not have spoken publicly about their lives. Being a Dalit (India's lowest possible caste, sometimes called Harijan, or Untouchable), Sabitri has lived her life being told she was the lowest of the low. And that her thoughts, her opinions, and her existence were of little consequence.

Dalits have been abused, raped, murdered, and thrown off land that is rightfully theirs. Despite "untouchability" being outlawed by the Constitution, Dalits are still treated like slaves by land-owners, and like criminals by the police. It was Gandhi who first called them "Harijans", meaning "the children of God", and called for greater equality. In Sabitri's state, Bihar,

however, the caste system is still very deeply entrenched.

The powerlessness into which Sabitri was born is mirrored by her present economic vulnerability. "We used to share-crop," Sabitri remembers. "We used to rent land from a landowner and pay for it with a share of the crops we grew. That was when we had the bullock to pull the plough. Without the bullock we can't farm the land."

The bullock went a few years ago, when Sabitri suddenly had to raise £40. Her daughter developed complications towards the end of a pregnancy, and needed an operation to save her life. The family had to borrow money to pay for the operation, and they are still paying interest on that debt. "The interest payments mean we'll probably have to sell the buffalo too," Sabitri says. Now landless, she and most of her family have to work as labourers, either on someone else's land, or at the local stone quarry.

Subitra Devi labouring in the quarry

photo: Achinto

but possible:

"Why have I joined this Association?" asks Nouhoum Coulibaly, a farmer from the Kelka zone, in Mali. "In one word — it has given me some *power:* power over our environment. Before, anyone could go to Mopti and get an official paper and come into our area to cut down wood. Helplessly, we watched outsiders cutting our wood, and there was nothing we could do. But now we have sat down with our local Forestry Commissioner, and agreed with him that outsiders will not be allowed to cut wood in our area. If they do try to, we can report them."

By Malian law, land and resources belong to the state, and official permission to cut wood has to be obtained from the local authorities. The trouble in Kelka was that anyone could get permission; there was no protection for local people's livelihoods, and therefore no incentive for farmers to manage the forests and replant trees.

Walde Kelka is an association of 13 villages who have been involved in a pioneering scheme in which management of natural resources has been devolved to local community level. Under the Kelka "constitution" each village recognises the right of others to manage their lands, on condition of respecting free access and usage rights. Now that the villages see themselves as owners of the lands, they are prepared to put much more effort into forest management. What happens in Kelka is now the business of the Kelka villages: they are the ones who depend on the forest and who therefore concern themselves with its preservation.

Nouhoum Coulibaly.
Beverley McAinsh

These developments in Kelka are indications of exciting new developments at national level in Mali, of new moves towards democracy and to devolving authority down to community level.

In 1991, violent conflicts in the streets of Mali's capital Bamako brought to an end 23 years of military dictatorship. When Alpha Oumar Konare became President the next year in the country's first democratic elections, he and his Alliance pour la Démocratie au Mali (ADEMA) faced the task of introducing genuinely democratic forms of government to a country where all idea of consensus and involvement had virtually disappeared. The dictatorship had been preceded by six years of centrally planned "African Socialism". Before that had been 60 years of French rule. Old ways of letting people's voices be heard, of devolving power over local resources, had been destroyed. The political disengagement and physical isolation of the majority of people — Mali is a huge and sparsely populated country — were recognised as serious problems for the new regime.

Rhéal Drisdelle, Oxfam's Representative in Mali, describes the early days of restoring democracy to the country: "the transitional government convened a National Conference in July/August 1991. Every group was represented, from the intellectuals to the farmers. It was a huge meeting and lasted three weeks. It was a unique moment in Malian history, a crossroads, at which people were asked 'What do you want? What is our collective vision for this country? Where should we go? How should we get there?'

"At that conference decentralisation very quickly became a major, major theme in discussions on the future direction of the country. It was agreed that decentralisation was the way to consolidate Malian democracy. This was how democracy would take hold within the communities, by having a decentralised government. They talk about 'the three Ds': democratisation, decentralisation, and development, which are seen as a whole."

Ousmane Sy, Head of the Decentralisation Mission, is the man charged with overseeing this process: "we're moving towards a system where local affairs will be controlled by elected local people. Today it is our duty to prepare all Malians for decentralisation — physically and intellectually. The state should act as a kind of referee to make sure that laws are not broken, but at the same time we need to create as wide an area of freedom and autonomy as possible."

Mali now has all the apparatus of a democracy: a dozen political parties, 25 small independent radio stations (one of them, in a particularly poor and remote area, funded by Oxfam), 40 independent newspapers, and an independent television station in the process of being set up.

"Yes," says Rhéal, "there will be corruption; yes, there will be mismanagement. You see, democratisation isn't something that happens at 9 o'clock one morning; it's a process that has to be visited again and again. But I think that the basic objective of bringing power out of a bunker in Bamako and into the communities will at least offer people — and especially the poorer people — the opportunity to play a role in the decisions which affect their lives."

Note: The newspaper, *Toguna*, is produced by an Oxfam-funded community association in Mali.

WHAT'S IN THIS ISSUE?

HOW OUR TAXES ARE SPENT! AT LEAST NOW, WE KNOW WHAT HAPPENS TO THEM!

Caught in the poverty trap

In their struggle to claim the rights they need, most poor people face the denial, not of one or two rights, but a whole inter-connected range of them. The following studies look at the complexity of the problems faced by poor people in three different continents. They show a multiple denial of rights leading to deepening poverty, and then on to the denial of further rights.

Legacies of conflict

Sok Sheuon, Suon Sea, and Phan Poeh all lived through one of the most savage episodes in human history, the dictatorship of Pol Pot, backed by his Khmer Rouge forces, in Cambodia. During those years, the most basic of rights were treated with complete contempt, and a million people died as a result.

Today, their rights have, in theory, been restored to Sok, Suon, and Phan: a sort of peace prevails in Cambodia. All three live, however, with the legacy of previous conflict, hampered in their atttempts to realise their basic rights by disability and the lasting damage that the Khmer Rouge caused to community structures and social trust. Continuing threats of violence undermine their efforts today to overcome the other problems facing them in an often hostile environment.

Livelihoods under threat

A few fish and frogs are all that Sok Sheuon survives on each week. This is all his two hectares of rice-field in Cambodia's Battambang province can provide. Having once promised him a livelihood and a plentiful supply of food, the land now often lies abandoned and under water, ruined by floods.

Sok is an amputee, having lost a leg when he stepped on a mine during the war. On returning to his home village in 1992, after the war, he found that all his family had been killed.

Sok Sheuon out fishing.

photo: Nic Dunlop

Coping with the trauma of the war and the loss of his family has been hard enough, but Sok also faces the struggle against the social stigma of being an amputee. To earn a living and gain independence, he rented some land in Kandal village, to grow rice. But this has only put him into debt.

"Everything I planted was lost in the floods. I can usually grow 20 bags of rice in one hectare. One bag usually lasts about half a month. For each hectare I also have to give three bags of rice as rent. I planted one or two mango and banana trees, but these also died in the floods."

Suon Sea, another mine victim, who lost both legs below the knee, also finds it difficult to gain a livelihood in post-war Cambodia: "In the refugee camp we didn't worry about food, as the Red Cross provided all that we needed. Here it is very hard to get an income. All our crops — rice, sugar cane, fruit trees — have been destroyed. We owe 20 dollars for rice, and we cannot now pay this back as our crop has failed. The money lender has allowed us to wait until next year to pay, but we are worried about the interest."

The war the world has forgotten

As far as the world is concerned, the Cambodian war has long since finished, but villagers in Battambang are still waiting for

Heng Moni Chenda.

photo: Nic Dunlop

peace. Khmer Rouge guerrillas are a constant threat to villages like Kandal. They carry out frequent raids on the village, stealing the little food and livestock that the villagers possess, or harassing families.

"Security is bad", says Suon Sea, "but the Khmer Rouge usually ignore us and go straight to the village centre. We feel frightened as there is often shooting."

The Khmer Rouge presence serves as a reminder of Pol Pot's genocidal regime. During his rule in the late 1970s, up to one million people were murdered. Pol Pot deliberately targeted trained personnel, destroying the country's services and infrastructure.

Heng Moni Chenda, director of Buddhism for Development, escaped from Cambodia in 1979 to a Thai border camp. "Under Pol Pot," he remembers, "all sense of community was destroyed. We had to live in communes imposed from the outside. People started to steal, to lie, to lose their sense of trust and community. Children denounced their parents. It was difficult just to survive."

Despite the presence of the UN's peace-keeping mission, the Khmer Rouge are still a force to be reckoned with. People who are trying to build a new life for themselves out of the country's ruins have to cope with the constant threat of violence from the guerrillas, and the hazards of land mines.

At least four million anti-personnel mines are scattered throughout the country, preventing many people from farming the land, and deterring displaced people from returning to their homes. Each month between 300 and 700 people need to have limbs amputated as a result of mine injuries.

From one generation to the next

Khmer Rouge terror has shaped the lives of Phan Poeh and his wife for over twenty years. Their very marriage — enforced by the Khmer Rouge back in 1976 — is a constant reminder of the days when Pol Pot was an absolute and bloody ruler of Cambodia.

But Phan Poeh's wife has been good to him: unlike the spouses of many amputees, she stayed with him after a landmine blew off his hand in 1983. "I was hunting for small animals to eat, when I saw it," he remembers. "I knew that it was dangerous, so I tried to remove it to protect others. It blew up in my hand."

Fifteen years after the defeat of Pol Pot, the Khmer Rouge still dominate Phan's life. His land has not been flooded like Suon Sea's, but he is unable to use the rice fields outside his village because the closeness of Khmer Rouge troops makes it too dangerous. His family has to depend on a few crops just round their house, and the chickens he is being helped to rear by a Cambodian organisation working with amputees in his village. He is unable to sleep at night because the Khmer Rouge come into the village as far as his house.

Phan's children do not go to school: they are hungry, and can't concentrate. Anyway, there is no money to pay for their schooling. "If I had my hand, I would be able to farm more easily, and then my children would have enough to eat, and we would be able to send them to school. Losing a hand is worse than losing a leg. At least if you lose a leg you can get a false one, which can make life slightly easier. Without a hand I cannot do many things."

What sort of future do Phan and his family face? "We do not want to move away from the Khmer Rouge," he says. "This is my home, I have always lived here. Anyway I do not know where is any free land elsewhere."

Training for local people in mine clearance, Battambang province, Cambodia.

photo: Nic Dunlop

Struggling to recover

The legacy of violence is incalculable for people like Sok, Suon, and Phan. It has left them with few resources, material or emotional, to cope with the ordinary business of survival and rebuilding, let alone a disaster like a flood.

"Integration has been difficult," says a Buddhist monk. "Most people still have no land, and those that do tend to live in heavily mined areas. Many still have no means of earning a living."

Free trade: whose freedom?

Alma Molina knows all about free trade. She lives and works in Mexico's free-trade border zone — described by one commentator as "a facsimile of hell on earth". Free trade for the 2,000 plus manufacturing plants there means the chance to maximise profits by pushing wages down to rock-bottom levels, and disregarding the environmental consequences of their operations.

For Alma free trade means a wage of $4.50 for a nine-hour day. It means working with dangerous chemicals without protective clothing. It means skin which is constantly stinging. And it means the sack for workers who try to organise to negotiate better conditions.

Through Alma's eyes

"I live in Juarez... In June 1992 I went to work for a US company with a plant in Juarez. I was among some 300 workers who make electrical switches and sensors. I earned the Mexican minimum wage of $4.50 for a nine-hour day.

"A group of us wanted to improve our working conditions, safety and wages at this company (Clarostat). We worked with dangerous chemicals, including phenol and epoxy resin, but no masks were provided. The chemicals irritated our skin.

"Six of us began to organise a union. We had meetings every two weeks. After a few months I was fired because I was trying to organise a union...

"Shortly after being fired, I was hired by Electro-componentes, which is a General Electric Company. The GE logo is on the factory. At that plant, 1800 workers make wiring for refrigerators sold in the US... I had been at GE for only seven days when I was called to the personnel office and shown a list with my name on it... The personnel man said that he did not know why my name was on the list, but that he would have to fire me anyway."

A cowed workforce

Wages in places like Juarez are less than a tenth of those paid in the US, and all the indications are that they will stay that way. The Mexican government, eager to attract new industry to Mexico, does its best to suppress the country's independent trade-union movement. Workers have few genuine safeguards against the abuses of employers.

For the largely female workforce in the free-trade zone, there is a stark choice: desperate poverty out in the countryside, a bitter struggle to survive unemployment in the shanty towns, or working for starvation wages in a General Motors or Du Pont manufacturing plant.

Ultimately, the transnational corporations hold the whip hand. They have already dealt a massive blow to many US workers by moving their manufacturing plants to Mexico. If Alma and her colleagues do achieve any success in their struggle for a fairer wage and safer working conditions, their victory could be a hollow one.

There are plenty more, even poorer, countries eager to woo the transnationals away from Mexico with yet greater tax and import concessions, and still harsher legislation to curb trade union activity.

In search of someone else's back yard

In the late 1980s California introduced more stringent state air-pollution controls. The result was almost immediate: a large-scale exodus of furniture manufacturers to Mexico's border zone. In one border town over a quarter of US firms with plants there said they had been attracted by the relative lack of environmental restrictions.

More than half the border zone plants produce hazardous waste: only a third comply with Mexico's toxic waste laws. Hundreds simply discharge heavy metals and other poisonous substances into open ditches. Much of that discharge is known to be associated with birth defects and brain damage: in towns in this area the incidence of anencephalic births (babies born without brains) is 30 times the Mexican average.

The American Medical Association has branded the whole region "a virtual cesspool and breeding ground for infectious diseases". Like the transnationals, such diseases do not let national boundaries get in their way: hepatitis and tuberculosis are now rife on both sides of the border.

Polluted water from factories being discharged into a river.
photo: Julio Etchart/Reportage

Toxic and industrial waste dumped by factories in the border zone.
photo: Julio Etchart/Reportage

Evading control

Mexico is part of the North America Free Trade Agreement, and there has been great concern over the social and environmental consequences of setting up the Agreement. As a result two subsidiary agreements have been negotiated, designed to curb abuses. Neither has been very successful:

* The labour agreement recognises the right to form and join trade unions, and to collective bargaining on wages and working conditions *but* any violations of these rights are to be "punished", not by trade sanctions, but by fact-finding exercises and consultations.

* The environment agreement has provided the resources to improve standards in Mexico, and recognises the need to establish acceptable minimum standards *but* the Commission set up to oversee the agreement has no powers of investigation and has to rely on evidence supplied by governments of offending countries. The responsibility for enforcing the agreement is also placed squarely on governments: the Mexican government does not even enforce its existing environmental laws.

An adequate livelihood and a safe environment are still remote prospects for Alma, her fellow-workers, and the children they may bear in years to come.

Struggling for a livelihood: Dorothy Chiredze's story

Historic inequality

In 1980 the newly independent Zimbabwe faced a legacy of deep inequality left by the previous white minority government. The white population made up about 5 per cent of the total population, but owned most of the country's wealth: its good agricultural land, its many rich mines, and its manufacturing industry.

The Land Act of 1930 had allocated over half the country's land to white settlers. They got the High Veldt, with its fertile soil and large river system. The remainder was left for the black population. Today, the situation has changed little: a mere 4,500 commercial farms, most of them still owned by white farmers, spread over the High Veldt. Meanwhile, four million black farmers are still crammed into the "Communal Areas" — the poorest quality land, fragile, heavily eroded, and in areas of low rainfall.

Farming in Zimbabwe's
Communal Areas.

photo: Chris Johnson

A fragile environment

Masvingo province in semi-arid southern Zimbabwe is a hostile
environment. Rainfall is low and erratic, and drought a regular
occurrence. Tree cover is almost non-existent. The scrubland is
largely bare, except for occasional colonies of mopane trees,
known locally as "the camels" because of their ability to survive
with little water.

During the long dry season the fragile top soil, unprotected
from the sun, bakes into a solid concrete-like crust. When the
rains come, that crust disintegrates and is transported through
the deep gullies which scar the land, into fast-flowing river
tributaries. These in turn feed into once-mighty rivers, like the
Tokwe and Runde, which carried Victorian explorers into the
interior. Now little more than streams for most of the year, they
are briefly transformed, during the rainy season, into torrents
which carry the soil from Masvingo down to the Indian Ocean.

A threatened lifestyle

Dorothy Chiredze lives in the village of Katule, which is typical
of many in Masvingo. She farms just over one hectare of land,
ploughing the soil with a hoe. In April, just before harvest, her
widely spaced, thin stalks of maize wilt in the sun. They are

nourished by water carried before dawn from a spring two hours' walk away.

If it is a good harvest, Dorothy will grow three sacks of maize. After she has sold one to pay for school fees, seeds for next year's harvest, oil, and other basic items, she will have enough left for herself, her two daughters, and one son, to last until January. Then she will have to work clearing land for wealthier neighbours, or on some larger commercial farms about ten kilometres away. Dorothy also grows small amounts of millet, which she brews into beer for cash, and some green vegetables.

The poorest families in Katule, most of them headed by women like Dorothy Chiredze, typically have less than two hectares of land, and no irrigation. What sets them apart from the wealthier people in the village, most of them say, is that they do not have cattle for ploughing. This restricts the area of land they are able to cultivate, and the amount of crops they can produce. Most cannot afford fertiliser, which explains why their maize stalks are smaller and paler than those of richer farmers. Few have savings or other assets, except a few goats, which they can sell to get through times of stress.

When disaster strikes

In a good year, the poorest families will grow enough maize to feed their families for three or four months. But many years are not good. The climate in Masvingo is changing, so farmers are less and less able to assess accurately when they need to plant. And the land is being hit by drought more frequently and more severely.

In 1992 Masvingo experienced the worst drought of the century. Almost the entire maize crop was destroyed, and most of the oxen died. Previous years of low rainfall and mediocre crops had already left people vulnerable: many had exhausted their savings or sold off assets like goats and chickens; some were already in debt.

In Dorothy's words

"It was the worst [drought] we had ever seen. Our maize was destroyed. We were left only with a little millet. Even those with much land lost their crops, so there was no work for us. There was emergency food, but it came so late ... There was much hunger in our villages, some children died from dysentery.

"My husband used to send money from Harare. He worked in a factory. But he came home because there was no more work.

"Our children ate only one meal each day. For many weeks we just had *sadza* (boiled maize meal) with no meat or vegetables. Our daughter became sick. The children were too weak to walk to school. Even if they were strong we did not

have enough money to send them because the school was charging higher fees. The school said they had no choice because the government was giving them less ..."

School students in Zimbabwe.

photo: Chris Johnson

Spiralling downwards

It takes only one, very small step to move from subsistence to hunger and starvation. Dorothy and her family have worked out a way of life that is perfectly viable, in a reasonable year. With their own small farm, their access to work on neighbouring larger farms, and the remittances from her husband in Harare, they have a whole strategy for survival carefully formulated. It is a strategy which works — just, and until things go wrong.

All too often, many things go wrong, at the same time. Then, vulnerable families like Dorothy's are trapped. When the rains failed, Dorothy and most of her neighbours had already lost the savings that might have tided them over. In an area where even the biggest farms for once had also lost their harvest, there was no labouring work to be had. Because Zimbabwe is heavily dependent on agriculture, the drought affected the whole economy, including its manufacturing industries. Economic recession led to massive factory lay-offs — and Dorothy found herself with an income less and an extra mouth to feed at home.

Not all the threats to the security of Dorothy's family came from the weather, or even from within Zimbabwe. The country's economic recession has been caused partly by its structural adjustment programme, as have the increased school fees Dorothy was unable to pay during the drought.

Once a family like Dorothy's start to slip downwards, it is difficult for it to start struggling upwards again. Dorothy's lack of savings or assets meant that her children became malnourished and ill; their ill health led to the disruption of their education. Poverty makes people less healthy, and so less productive, and then in turn still poorer and less healthy: it's a simple but utterly vicious circle.

An uncertain future

"This year we will have a small harvest. We could not buy seed or fertiliser, and we have planted less. There was no money to hire an ox, so I ploughed the land by hand. If the rains are good, maybe we will grow two bags of maize; in a good year we used to grow three. I will have to work on the farms of others for food maybe as early as December.

"If the rains are bad again, I don't know if we will survive. We pray for rain ... but life is hard. We struggle to stay alive, but life is so hard."

The drought of 1992 did more than leave Dorothy's family hungry that year. It undermined their whole future. Because it left them poorer, they were unable to make the best use of their land when the rains returned, so their harvest will be smaller than it might otherwise have been. And that will have repercussions on the next year's crop, because Dorothy will have to spend more time working on the farms of her wealthier neighbours and less on her own farm.

Meanwhile the future looks unpromising for Dorothy's children. They have already had a year's schooling disrupted. With school fees increasing, and their family's income decreasing, there will probably be more disruptions in the future. Besides, with Dorothy off working for someone else, their labour will be needed more on their own land.

Poverty is transmitted down through the generations, just as wealth is; unless action is taken rapidly to enable Dorothy and her family to secure the rights to which they are entitled, her children seem to have little chance of escaping the poverty which has trapped their parents.

Drought in Zimbabwe, 1992

photo: Greg Williams

On 26 January 1950 we are going to enter into a life of contradictions. In politics we will be recognising the principle of one man [sic] one vote, and one vote one value. In our social and economic life, we shall ... continue to deny the principle of one man one value ... How long should we continue to deny equality in our social and economic life? ... we will do so only by putting our political democracy in peril.

from Dr Ambedkar's speech to the Indian Constituent Assembly, November 1949

An agenda for change

If present trends are allowed to continue unchallenged, the future is a frightening prospect. It will be a world of deep divisions, of societies segregated between the "haves" and the "have-nots": between those with skills and opportunities, jobs and wealth, and those with none; between those who "count" in economic, social, and political terms, and those who do not.

This is a prescription for increasing misery and deepening instability. The only way out is to tackle poverty and injustice, so that all people have a stake in society. We all have a responsibility to engage in that struggle, to turn the words of innumerable international covenants, agreements, and declarations — all venerated, often ignored — into action.

Because rights are so interlinked and interdependent, it is only part of the solution to consider them separately, and look at ways of safeguarding each one individually. Instead, we have to plan for a world where the *whole body* of basic rights is recognised and put into place. Let us look at the sort of world environment where those rights could become reality, and consider what needs to be done to create such an environment.

Opportunity

Poor men and women are ready to seize the opportunities which come their way. But they can only make the best use of these opportunities if they are able to meet their most basic needs: they must have enough to eat, clean water to drink and wash in, health care, education, a home, political freedom, and freedom from violence.

A healthy, well-fed, educated population is likely to be an economically effective one, so money invested by governments in the health and education of their people is money well spent. Yet in country after country governments are cutting back on state spending, and demanding that people start paying for services which have been free in the past.

Lakhi, of Birganj, Bangladesh, reads the article she has written for her community association magazine. "I have written about how we women have worked hard to create a better social and economic life for ourselves."

photo: Shafiqul Alam

All too often, the result is children having to be withdrawn from school, and people going without the medical treatment they need. Women are particularly hard hit by these developments: they face more health risks themselves, and they are now being expected to provide free care for sick members of their families. Girls are usually the first to be withdrawn from school when times are hard.

All governments must take responsibility for providing essential services, such as health care and education. In particular, they should:

- allocate at least 20 per cent of all government spending to providing the services which poor people need most, including primary health care, primary education, clean water and sanitation;
- provide primary health care and basic education free of charge.

All governments must greatly reduce military spending, investing in people rather than death and destruction.

Aid donors must increase the percentage of their country's wealth going on aid to poor countries.

The UN target is 0.7 per cent. Donor governments must agree timetables for reaching that target.

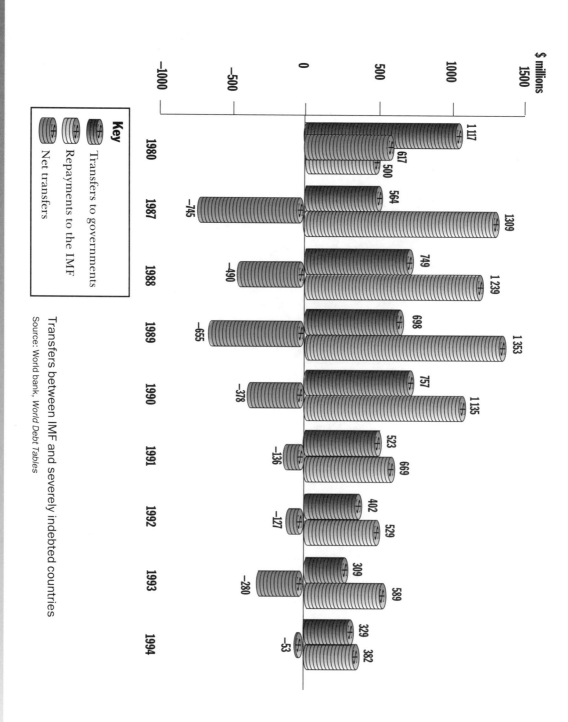

$ millions

| | 1980 | 1987 | 1988 | 1989 | 1990 | 1991 | 1992 | 1993 | 1994 |

Key

Transfers to governments

Repayments to the IMF

Net transfers

Transfers between IMF and severely indebted countries

Source: World bank, World Debt Tables

Creditor governments and international financial institutions must act to reduce the debts of the most severely indebted low-income countries.

A co-ordinated debt-relief strategy, setting out improved terms, should be drawn up. This would include writing off 80-100 per cent of debts owed to Paris Club countries. Agreement is needed on new measures, to tackle the growing crisis of debts owed to multilateral institutions such as the World Bank and the IMF; these measures would need to be financed from within those institutions.

Participation

Democracy can take many different forms, but if it is to flourish in a healthy society, people must have a say, within their own household, as well as locally, nationally, and internationally, in the issues and policies which affect their lives. Governments must be open in their dealings and accountable to the people they govern. There must be respect at all levels for the rule of law, and for the civil and political rights of all individuals.

Some governments treat democratic rights as luxuries that their country can indulge in at some, usually ill-defined, time in the future, when economic growth is safely under way. But repression and economic growth do not necessarily go hand-in-hand; economic growth without a respect for people's democratic rights is unlikely to be sustainable.

Demonstrating for democracy, Port-au-Prince, Haiti.

photo: Jenny Matthews

Average for selected developed countries 215 papers

How electorates keep themselves informed: daily newspapers per 500 inhabitants in rich and poor countries

Source: UNESCO

Average for selected developing countries 0.4 papers

All governments must take measures to strengthen their countries' democratic institutions, from village associations to an independent judiciary.

Institutions at local, national and international level must be democratic, transparent in their dealings, and accountable to the people they exist to serve.

A fair distribution of wealth and power

A system where large numbers of people are excluded from the benefits of economic growth is not merely unjust: it is inefficient, and the growth is unlikely to last. In particular, no nation can genuinely claim to be "developing" if half its population — its women — are disadvantaged and marginalised, cut off from the advantages of that development.

At an international level, many features of trading patterns — low prices for raw commodities, protectionist trade barriers, the unrestrained powers of transnational corporations, and irresponsible use of natural resources — act against the interests of poorer countries. For these countries, such patterns are leading to economic decline and environmental destruction.

In countries where land ownership is very unequal, and a more equal allocation would make a significant contribution to the reduction of poverty, land must be redistributed in favour of poor men and women.

The interests of poor producers must be protected at local and national levels.

They must be able to obtain loans on favourable terms, advice about marketing their produce, and training.

Harvest-time in northern Vietnam

photo: Keith Bernstein

All forms of discrimination against women must be outlawed.

In particular, they must enjoy the same rights as men to:
* own and inherit land;
* obtain the resources they need to make a living;
* obtain loans;
* join trade unions and other campaigning and development groups.

    They must also have the right to equal pay with men and to maternity leave and job protection during and after pregnancy.

The World Bank must do more to eradicate poverty by:

* involving community-based organisations, women's groups, and non-government organisations in the design of economic reforms;
* doing more to protect basic services for poor people, such as health care and education, and insisting that governments stop charging fees to those using them;

- putting less emphasis on deregulated markets, and more on the fair distribution of wealth and power, and on regulating markets in the interests of poor producers and consumers.

World trade systems must be reformed, to generate wealth for the many, not just the few.

- Poor producers must receive fair prices for the commodities they make or cultivate;
- Trade barriers put up against developing countries must be dismantled.
- Rich countries must stop dumping subsidised exports to poor countries.

Consumers must enable small producers to obtain a fair price for their labour.

They should buy Fair Trade goods wherever possible and put pressure on retailers and suppliers to make more Fair Trade goods available.

Peace and security

There is no greater challenge facing the international community than that of creating the conditions for peace and security. There can be no lasting peace without a reduction in poverty. But without peace, efforts to eradicate poverty will fail.

Conflict, violence, and crime are being fuelled by poverty, the widening gap between haves and have-nots, and the suppression of minority social and ethnic groups. Civilians, particularly poor women and children, are bearing the brunt of that violence. Family and community networks are being destroyed, and livelihoods wrecked.

Ultimately, it is individual societies that will have to create the conditions for greater peace and security. Only increased opportunity and participation for all, with a more just distribution of wealth and power, will bring a permanent end to conflict.

The international community is still searching for the appropriate response to conflict. There is a desperate need to identify the most useful role that outside parties can play when violence and armed conflict break out.

Member governments must strengthen the UN's capacity to prevent and resolve armed conflict, quickly and effectively.

They must:
- set up a permanent rapid deployment force, ready to be sent instantly to conflict zones;
- send monitors promptly to investigate large-scale human rights abuses;

- provide the financial support the UN needs to be an effective peace-keeping force.

The international community must help countries which are rebuilding after war and conflict.

Reconstruction efforts must:
- address the underlying causes of the conflict;
- create conditions for lasting peace;
- involve existing organisations and structures in the reconstruction process, and enable the people affected to participate fully in its design and implementation.

A high-level expert committee must be created, reporting to the UN Secretary-General, to look at ways of controlling and reducing the international arms trade.

In particular, there must be a comprehensive and worldwide ban on the manufacture, stockpiling, export, and use of anti-personnel landmines.

A safe environment

Poverty is a major destroyer of the environment since poor people often have no alternative but to damage and overuse local resources such as forests and farmland. All too often, they have very little realistic choice, even though they may be painfully aware of the extent to which they are prejudicing their own futures.

In the rich industrialised world, considerably more choice is available to most people. And it is here that the bulk of the damage is being done to the global environment. The impact of high levels of energy consumption and wasteful life-styles in rich countries is felt far beyond their national boundaries.

Rich industrialised countries must examine the impact their activities are having on the environment, especially their energy use and agricultural practices.

Rich industrialised countries must demonstrate their commitment to the Rio Earth Summit Agenda 21 recommendations.

They should provide the additional finance needed to implement them, and environment-friendly technological know-how.

Farmer from Nyasa province, Mozambique, standing by the new pig-stye he has just built. People can plan for the future now that peace and stability have returned to the country.

photo: Matthew Chambers

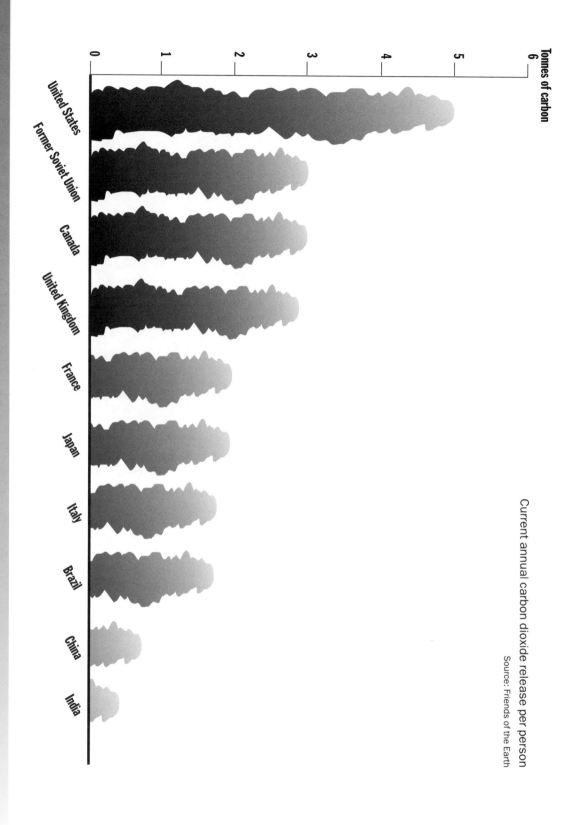

Tonnes of carbon

0 1 2 3 4 5 6

United States
Former Soviet Union
Canada
United Kingdom
France
Japan
Italy
Brazil
China
India

Current annual carbon dioxide release per person

Source: Friends of the Earth

Industrialised countries must introduce measures to reduce their own energy use.

These measures should include:
- tougher energy-efficiency standards;
- building-insulation programmes;
- investment in renewable energy sources, such as solar or wind power;
- tax penalties for over-exploitation of natural resources.

Rich industrialised countries must commit themselves to reduce carbon dioxide emissions by 30 per cent from 1990 levels by 2005.

Individuals and groups in rich industrialised countries must act locally to protect their environment.

In particular they should conserve energy and recycle resources themselves, and campaign for energy to be conserved and resources recycled wherever possible in their locality.

Children at a primary school in Ky Anh district, Vietnam, working in their school's tree nursery.

photo: Sean Sprague

The issues outlined above are the ones that the Oxfam Campaign will be focusing on in the coming months and years. The list may seem an ambitious one but, as we have seen, all these changes are possible, given the political and moral will to achieve them. Many of the changes and reforms outlined will take time to achieve: things cannot change overnight. But the important point is that progress should *begin*, and begin in the right direction.

Note: The full list of Oxfam's recommendations can be found in Chapter 7 of *The Oxfam Poverty Report*.

Campaigning for change

All over the world, people are proving that old patterns and ways of running things can be changed, and that hunger, poverty, and powerlessness are not inevitable. They are demanding, and obtaining, a realisation of their rights in ways that might have seemed unthinkable to their parents or grandparents — or even, once, to themselves.

And their efforts are being mirrored by the campaigning actions of people in the world's affluent countries: people who know that it is morally wrong for their own prosperity to be paid for by depriving others of their basic rights; people who understand that there can be no genuine or lasting security for anyone in a world where one person in four is denied the most basic of rights; people who are prepared to turn their concerns into effective action.

Some of this action happens out in the community: visits to MPs, organising petitions. Some takes the form of dialogue between staff from organisations such as Oxfam and senior officials from the world's governments or international financial institutions. Wherever and however it takes place, people are most likely to be effective when their convictions are based on clear, accurate information and on respect for the understanding and achievements of the people for whose rights they are campaigning.

Showing the way

Rosangela lives in a hot, one-roomed shack in the *favela*, or shanty town, of Beira Rio in Recife, Brazil. The shanty town is a maze of narrow, wooden walkways and tiny make-shift homes, suspended precariously above an old mangrove swamp. Live electricity wires dangle overhead; below, the wood is rotten, and gaping holes reveal steaming sewage in the water. Yet behind the *favela* lies a large plot of dry land, which is completely unused. It belongs to the military, and the residents of Beira Rio dare not build houses on it for fear of being roughly evicted.

Built on a swamp, the *favela* is particularly prone to rats. Rosangela, along with the Residents' Association, has been involved in lobbying the council to get rid of them. "I found two dead rats under my cooker. There were times when I couldn't sleep — there were rats scuttling around on the floor and in my saucepans. We managed to persuade the council to lay down poison, and since then we haven't seen any rats."

The gap between rich and poor in Brazil is one of the most pronounced in the world. Its huge wealth is concentrated in the hands of a small number of powerful people, those who gained most from the military government's "economic miracle" of the 1960s and 1970s. Out in the countryside 44 per cent of the land (and most of the cultivable land) is owned by just 1 per cent of the population; 67 per cent of landholders occupy just 6 per cent. Brazil is the world's second-largest agricultural exporter, but, in 1994, more than 32 million people, out of a population of 154 million, were living in absolute poverty. One-third of all Brazilians do not have enough to eat, and malnutrition causes seven out of ten deaths among children under five.

Rosangela washing up in the alley outside her home.

photo: Steve Andrews

On an income of six dollars a day for doing washing and cleaning jobs, Rosangela is pretty near the bottom of the heap. But, luckily, Beira Rio now has a very active Residents' Association, which in turn is part of one of the most dynamic anti-poverty movements in the world today: the Hunger Campaign.

The Campaign aims to motivate Brazilian citizens to tackle the poverty in their country. Rich and poor, young and old, bankers, computer programmers, shop-keepers, and cleaners are all getting involved: some do house-to-house collections, or contribute part of their salary, others donate luncheon vouchers. 4,500 inmates in nine prisons in Rio de Janeiro fasted, in solidarity, for the Campaign, and were able to donate their missed meals (about 2.5 tons of food) to feed 200 families for two weeks.

"We couldn't wait for the state to act," says Vando Nogueiro, a former Campaign coordinator in Recife, "so we decided to try to meet people's most immediate needs, and then try to deal with poverty on a more permanent basis."

Beira Rio is one of many areas which is now able to run a community soup-kitchen, thanks to the support of the Hunger

Ediasusa Maria do Santo, Vice-President of Beira Rio Residents' Association. "We are discussing setting up a community school, to fill the gap in the school timetable in the middle of the day. It could help children who have problems learning to read."

photo: Steve Andrews

Campaign, and the work of volunteers like Rosangela. But soup-kitchens are just a beginning; their main value is as a means of encouraging poor communities to organise themselves and demand their basic rights. With the help of the Campaign, the Residents' Association has publicised the district's rat problem, and pressurised the local council into taking action. Now they are campaigning to move to a new, dry site.

Media interest about the Campaign has been huge, helping to raise public awareness about the extent of poverty, and putting it firmly on the political agenda. As a result, in the recent general election, combating hunger featured in the manifestos of every election candidate.

Campaign activists believe hunger is basically a political problem. "In 1989 Brazil produced 58 million tonnes of grain," Vando points out. "In 1994 that was up to 74 million tonnes. And 58 million tonnes is enough to give every Brazilian 3,500 calories per day. An adult only needs 2,500 calories, so you can see the cause of starvation in Brazil is not a lack of food. This year we intend to start discussing agricultural reform. We will lose friends because it's a harder nut to crack — people's personal interests are at stake. The root causes of poverty are so visible it's not hard to talk about them; what is hard is to tackle them."

The Hunger Campaign is a new way of addressing these explosive political issues, by mobilising the concern of ordinary people. "It's a creative way of harnessing the desire of citizens to do away with hunger. We want one citizen to show solidarity with another citizen."

Miguel Anacleto, a computer programmer with the Bank of Brazil, and the co-ordinator of a group working with Indian community organisations, has a still wider vision. "My vision is of links between people of the world that cut across government boundaries. My vision is of independent people showing solidarity."

Sharing the struggle

Paying a fair price

Justino Peck lives with his wife, Cristina, and three children in a small, simple cabin in San Jose, Belize, Central America. Electricity has not yet reached their remote village, so for light they use kerosene lamps, made from instant coffee bottles with cotton cloth for wicks. A nearby hand-pump provides clean water. They cook over an open fire on the floor.

Their main source of income is cocoa beans. Planting and tending the cacao trees, and harvesting the beans, is hard work, and the farmers also have to transport their crop themselves to the warehouse in Punta Gorda. For Justino this means carrying a 100 pound sack of cocoa beans on his back across two miles of rough, frequently wet, terrain to the road, and then taking a two-hour trip by bus.

Nevertheless, until the early 1990s Justino and his family lived simply but comfortably. They were able to buy clothes and basic necessities, and enjoy a varied diet. But their security and

Justino Peck, in the UK for the launch of Maya Gold chocolate.

photo: James Hawkins

91

comfort came to an end when the price of cocoa fell dramatically between 1992 and 1993. At a mere 22 pence a pound, less than half its former value, the crop was not even worth harvesting: they simply left it to rot. Stifled by weeds, the trees stood testimony to the plight of the farmers, and to the precariousness of livelihoods which depend on fluctuating world market prices.

Just before prices fell, the farmers of San Jose had set up a co-operative to transport and market their beans, with Justino as chair. They had taken out a loan so that they could pay farmers on delivery for their crops. But, with prices so low, they failed to attract many farmers and soon fell behind with their loan repayments.

The future looked bleak, when the group was approached by Green and Black's, a UK chocolate company, who wanted to buy their cocoa for their new Fair Trade "Maya Gold" chocolate. The company offered well above market price, at 48 pence per pound, and gave them a three-year guarantee to buy all they could produce.

With improved prices and a long-term trading commitment, the farmers now have an assurance that their hard work will be rewarded. Many local farmers who had abandoned their farms and emigrated in search of paid work are going back to their villages and their traditional work.

Florence Muhindo picking coffee in Uganda. Florence is poor because the price she gets for coffee is so low. She is one of millions kept poor by unfair patterns of trade.

photo: Geoff Sayer

Consumer power in action

Not so many years ago people like Justino and Florence might as well have lived on a different planet as far as the rich world's chocolate eaters and coffee drinkers were concerned. Most UK consumers had only one aim: to pay as low a price as possible for the goods in their supermarket trolleys. The people who had grown the crops on which their comfort and convenience depended were shadowy figures half a world away, cogs in the mighty machine of international trade.

Today things are beginning to change. These Oxfam campaigners, like Justino, are part of a new movement, a movement that may, in time, revolutionise the way we go about our shopping.

Oxfam was one of the pioneers of the Fair Trade movement. Since the 1960s it has been buying crafts and food at a fair price from low-income Third World producers, and selling them through its shops and mail-order catalogue. Now it has moved on, with other agencies, to actively promoting the whole Fair Trade message.

Oxfam campaigners have helped to take that message right out into their communities: they have pressurised supermarkets to stock Fair Trade products like Cafédirect coffee, Clipper tea, and

Fair Trade campaigning in Croydon.

photo: Brian Beardwood

Preparing for an Oxfam
Cafédirect tasting.

photo: Oxfam

"It's fun, the public like a free cup of coffee, and most seem genuinely interested in Fair Trade."

"Response to Cafédirect was entirely favourable. It's much easier to stop people if you have something to show them while they're talking to you."

"You can ask questions and complete surveys as they taste it, and then ask them to take action."

Maya Gold chocolate; they have urged consumers to buy — and demand — these products.

They have also taken the message to decision-makers. It was partly because of letters written by Oxfam supporters to the Ministry of Agriculture that proposed changes to the trade rules of the European Union were modified; changes affecting the livings of banana growers in the Windward Islands have been phased in more gradually than originally intended, to give them more time to adjust to increased competition.

Fair Trade campaigners have often found that they are pushing at an open door. The surveys they have conducted reveal shoppers overwhelmingly in favour of Fair Trade: 85 per cent of people surveyed have said they would like to see more Fair Trade products in their supermarkets. Within three years of its launch in 1991 a million jars of Cafédirect coffee had been sold. Price, of course, is still important, but for many people there is now a new dimension to shopping: the effect their decisions can have on poor producers thousands of miles away.

It is a message which the supermarkets are now listening to. Most of the big chains are consulting with organisations like the Fairtrade Foundation, and Sainsburys now get more letters on Fair Trade than on the length of their check-out queues! The buyer for the Edinburgh Safeway store reported that he had more favourable comments when he introduced Cafédirect than for any other product he had ever introduced. New lines are being developed: Cafédirect instant coffee was launched in early 1994.

People-friendly shopping seems to be here to stay, and Oxfam campaigners are helping the momentum of what could become an unstoppable force.

Thinking globally: acting locally

... in Manchester

Few things have shocked the world more in recent years than the 1994 Rwanda massacres. In Manchester, local campaigners provided the means for the horror of local people to be translated into rapid and effective help. Then, as the TV cameras, inevitably, moved on to the next story, they helped to keep Rwanda's tragedy in the minds of ordinary Mancunians.

Within days of the first outbreaks of violence in Rwanda, they had helped staff from Oxfam's Emergency Unit to erect a giant water storage tank, identical to those used in emergency situations, in central Manchester. Shoppers and office-workers were offered the chance to "buy" a cup of water — a familiar enough situation for most refugees, but never experienced

Water equipment from the People's Plane begins the second leg of its journey.

photo: Pete Brabban

before by the citizens of Chorlton or Levenshulme. Civic leaders, politicians, religious leaders, a local actress, and children from local schools all helped to draw attention to the tank, and badger the public for money.

So generous was the response that within days £220,000 had been raised, enough to charter a plane and fill it with emergency supplies for Rwanda. The North-West People's Plane was one of eight funded and organised by Oxfam campaigners throughout the UK, and it left Newcastle for Goma, Zaire, on 12 August.

Manchester's campaigners were convinced their job was not over. They were determined to keep the issue live, but, like most local media, Manchester papers were interested only in news with a Manchester angle. Which is why the media turned out in force for a simple, but deeply moving, ceremony organised by local Oxfam campaigners in central Manchester's Peace Gardens: the planting of 20 forget-me-not plants.

... in Oxford

A similar problem faced the Oxford Oxfam Group when they tried to interest local media in the Rwanda tragedy. "Why should people in Oxford be worried about what's happening in Rwanda?" asked one journalist. "We tried to convince him that this was a moral issue, that Rwandans are people like us," remembers group member Joanna Gill. "We asked him what he thought people in Oxford would do if a similar horror hit us here. He was sceptical, but there was plenty of proof that people here *do* care. In just five months we raised over £6,000 from street collections, vigils, and collections in local pubs and theatres. And the local media came to recognise this concern — the Oxford Mail ran a special appeal on our behalf, and raised a further £6,000. A peaceful, affluent small city like Oxford is a world away from the Goma refugee camps, but people here did want to help."

Oxford is a world away, too, from the minefields of Cambodia or Mozambique. And, since they are countries which no longer hit even the national dailies, few people in Oxford know about the damage still being caused by mines: the men, women, and children who tread on them and lose their legs, their arms, their sight or their lives; the land that even hungry people do not dare to cultivate because they know it has been sown with mines.

When people do know the facts, they are appalled. "We collected over a hundred signatures to the anti-mines petition in just a couple of hours," says Joanna. "We set up a stall in town, and people were keen to sign. We were helped by a very good band busking just next to us. Once they knew what we were doing, they were all for us. Everyone who stopped to listen to them was told to come over and sign our petition. And they did."

Influencing the decision-makers

Vigil for Rwanda at the
Martyrs' Memorial, Oxford.

photo: Bob Crampton

The Campaigns Network

"The pen is mightier than the sword." Well, maybe; maybe not.
But a carefully thought out, well-reasoned letter is still a
powerful weapon in the struggle for people's basic rights.
Oxfam's Campaigns Network is made up of some 5,000 people
who are prepared, first, to master the complexities and details of
a whole range of issues, and, then, to put pen to paper or fingers
to keyboards.

Quarterly newsletters keep them up to date with world
events as they are affecting poor people in the countries where
Oxfam works, and suggest concerns they might want to bring to
the attention of decision-makers. These campaigners aim high,
writing to their MPs when appropriate, but thinking nothing of
tackling the Chairman of Tesco, the Prime Minister, or the
President of the World Bank. So their letters have to be well
informed, not open to being rejected out of hand because of
details not considered.

"When Oxfam ran its Africa: Make or Break campaign," says
Mark Luetchford, the Network Coordinator, "we had two main
rallying cries: raise the aid, and cut the debt. They were simple,
powerful, demands, which we knew would make a huge

Ian Hislop and Angus Deayton delivering letters to 10 Downing Street, with a cardboard cut-out of PM John Major. Some 30,000 letters from Oxfam campaigners expressed concern over threats to Africa's recovery.

photo: Andrew Simms

difference to people in Africa, and which people felt confident in outlining. But Networkers were also able to make more informed demands. They were able to write to people in power about the Trinidad Terms, and the virtues of selling off IMF gold stocks to fund debt write-offs. They could quote statistics and trends when lobbying the Prime Minister about proposed aid cuts."

The approach worked. The aid budget was frozen rather than cut in 1993; the freeze continued into 1994, but with promises of extra funds being made available in 1995. As for debt, Kenneth Clarke is currently pushing plans for debt reduction at G7 summits very similar to those proposed by Oxfam Networkers.

Other Network initiatives have had even more success. Tuzla airport was reopened in March 1994 for the passage of relief goods after Network members bombarded the Prime Minister with letters asking Britain to use its influence as a Permanent Member of the Security Council. Ten days after the Network started a letter-writing campaign to the Foreign Office in 1994 calling for a ban on landmines, the UK government announced a restricted ban on British exports of landmines which do not self-destruct or self-neutralise. Foreign Office sources acknowledged the influence of "a certain letter-writing campaign".

"In all modesty," says Mark, "we can't be sure that it was our campaign that made all the difference. But, judging by the dates, our campaign must at the very least have added weight to other ones. Anyway, we're certainly keeping the pressure up. We're now asking Networkers to keep writing to the Prime Minister, urging him to work for a total, worldwide ban on the production, stockpiling, sale, and use of *all* anti-personnel mines."

"Come on, John," wrote one campaigner, R. Whitmore, "Africa's people are getting poorer. Raise the aid. Cut the debt."

Constituency contacts

Some of Oxfam's most effective campaigners are the ones who have opened a direct route from the towns and villages where they live, right into the corridors of power. There are few better ways of helping to create the political will for change than by talking to MPs in the places where they have to listen — their own constituencies.

Prime Ministers, Foreign Secretaries, Chancellors of the Exchequer — all need to show that they care about the concerns of local voters. Any one of their constituents can ask for a meeting or turn up to one of their regular surgeries, and be virtually sure that they will listen. The humblest back-bencher, too, has an ear which is worth bending, and a vested interest in listening to his or her constituents.

Oxfam campaigners have been doing this for years, putting their case informally to their MPs on a huge range of issues, from Cambodia, to overseas aid budgets, to VAT on Oxfam shop donated goods. Because face-to-face discussion is such an effective way of interesting, involving, and convincing people in power, Oxfam is now developing an organised network of constituency contacts.

Each contact (eventually most constituencies will have at least one) undertakes to visit their MP, alone or with a small group, at least twice a year. Bob Hammond, for example, lives in the Nottinghamshire constituency of Rushcliffe. "I visit my MP — currently Kenneth Clarke — at his surgery," says Bob, "and I usually have 10 to 15 minutes with him. Because of his Cabinet duties, he only holds surgeries once a month, making do with letters at other times. Nevertheless, we have struck up what I regard as a healthy rapport: he listens to what I have to say, clearly respects the work of Oxfam and responds positively both in our meetings and in correspondence, even when we have to agree to differ over policies being pursued by the government."

A busy MP, in even the most marginal constituency, will only pay this sort of attention to a well-informed constituent, who has come prepared with carefully marshalled arguments. Twice a year Oxfam produces an *Action Guide*, which contacts can use to supplement the information they are already obtaining from the media.

By its very nature, the contact network is a small-scale operation, but it is a powerful one. It is enabling "the Third World case" to be put to some of the most influential people in the country by people whose views have to matter to them.

Getting in where the action is

"'You've got five minutes, between the Bootleg Beatles and the Saw Doctors,' they told me. Five minutes, I thought — more like 30 seconds, given the attention span right now of this lot. It was Sunday afternoon after all, so most of them had already been there for three days, absorbing the atmosphere — and who knows what else ... Get it all into the first two minutes, I told myself, or you'll have lost them.

"So there's the sun blazing down, and there are 100,000 people *at least* standing sweating in front of me. Then the organisers said 'You're on', and I just boogied on to the stage, spread my arms out wide like Madonna, and yelled into the mike 'Good afternoon Glastonbury!'

"'Guess who got the short straw?' I shouted. 'I've got less than five minutes to talk to you about world poverty. So where on earth do you start? You start with the basics, that's where you start. Basic rights. With Oxfam's Campaign for basic rights for people.

"'Why are they basic? Because they're things you and I take for granted: enough food, clean water, shelter, a say in your future — simple things like that. Why do we call them rights? Because the world's governments have agreed to them. Ratified them. Agreed they're not luxuries but rights. In theory. But one in four people in today's world lives in absolute poverty.

"'Basic rights', I said, 'are not luxuries — they make the difference between mere survival and really living. You might not want to change your life, and that's OK. But speak out against injustice. Use your voice, and you can change someone else's life. Join Oxfam's campaign for basic rights, and please sign our charter.'

"Well, as I came off the stage, there was this huge cheer, and when I was giving the mike back to the organiser I said 'Who's just walked on?' 'That was for you,' they said. I heard afterwards that people had been coming out saying 'OK, this Charter I'm signing — where is it?'

"I rang my mum later, and said 'Mum, I've just had 100,000 people at Glastonbury listening to me talking about world poverty. And cheering me.' My mum's reaction was: 'you never stood up in front of 100,000 people when you hadn't had a shower for three days? — you must have been filthy. What will people think?' 'Don't worry, mum,' I told her, 'I was just a tiny distant pinhead to most of them.' 'Well maybe', she said, 'but did they read your name out?'"

After her spectacular Glastonbury debut, Julie Harrington learnt that 4,000 people had signed the giant Basic Rights Charter in the Oxfam Campaign festival tent.

Glastonbury revellers signing Oxfam's Basic Rights Charter.

photo: Julie Harrington

Influencing the influencers

Joining forces for change

"I knew about our poverty and suffering," said Solofina Daka, an elderly grandmother. "And we have made enormous efforts to overcome it. But this workshop has opened my eyes fully. The problems we face are not just due to the causes in our own

Enoch Samudengo writing his letter.

photo: Oxfam

villages and among us, but the ones coming from beyond the borders of Zambia."

Solofina was speaking at a meeting of Oxfam partner organisations in Zambia's Eastern Province. Like others at the meeting, she was voicing her anger and frustration at the effect on her life of decisions taken far away by the World Bank and the International Monetary Fund.

And, like others there, Solofina resolved that she would be silent and unheard no longer, that she would write to the world's finance ministers, telling them what the policies of the IMF meant to her in her daily life.

The letter-writing campaign which began at that meeting was taken up in the months that followed by 15,000 other Zambians, as well as by many people in other African countries. Oxfam supported the campaign by providing basic materials, such as pens and stationery pads, and by helping groups to organise meetings at which people could discuss what they wanted to say.

"I don't think I will ever be employed," wrote Jones Katongo Bwalya. "When structural adjustment was introduced, we were told it will improve our life, there will be more jobs. All I see is more workers losing jobs. Our lives are becoming nothing short of slavery."

The visit of Lucy Muyoyeta, Oxfam's Zambia Representative, to present the letters from Africa to Kenneth Clarke, UK Chancellor of the Exchequer, at the September 1993 meeting of the IMF was more than a protest about the Fund's structural adjustment policies: for the first time poor people in Africa were directly addressing the institutions which control their countries' economies; for the first time, Oxfam was campaigning, not just *for* them, but *with* them.

This massive African initiative has been matched by the efforts of individuals and groups in the UK; the letters from Africa have not been the only ones to reach Kenneth Clarke on the subject of the continent's debt problem. In fact he received so many letters about debt relief for Uganda that HM Treasury had to get special reply postcards printed. When the matter was brought up in Parliament, MPs referred to massive concern on the matter among their constituents.

The combined persuasion of African and UK campaigners has undoubtedly had its effect on the British government. Kenneth Clarke backed Oxfam's call for debt relief for Africa at the IMF/World Bank meetings in autumn 1993. In autumn 1994 the leaders of the seven largest industrialised nations (the Group of Seven or G7) agreed to consider more lenient terms for rescheduling and writing off debts owed to them.

Then in early 1995 Western governments agreed to a new debt-reduction package, under which the poorest countries could reduce their debt by two-thirds. It was a welcome initiative, and the first reaction of campaigners was one of jubilation. It looked as if Uganda, the first country to be granted the new terms, was about to have 67 per cent of its vast debt written off. Closer scrutiny, however, showed that the new arrangements still do not, in Oxfam's view, go far enough. Complicated rules, set by creditor governments, mean that debts contracted after a specified date are not eligible for reduction. More importantly, debt owed to the World Bank and the IMF cannot be reduced. In the end only 6 per cent of Uganda's debt was written off.

Nevertheless, the new terms do represent an important step forward. A mere two years previously, Oxfam campaigners had been assured that it was completely crazy even to suggest that debts owed to World Bank and IMF should be reduced. Today, there is widespread acknowledgement among the governments of the G7 nations that action is needed. The 1995 package seems likely to be just the first step of a longer process. More and more, apparently impenetrable institutions like the IMF and World Bank are showing that they are susceptible to public pressure, particularly when it is informed by concrete experience of problems in debtor countries, and applied by people from both rich and poor countries working together.

Lucy Moyoyeta presenting letters from Africa to Kenneth Clarke, in New York for an IMF meeting.
photo: Dennis Brock

Moving forward — together

Oxfam's Campaign, *Together for Rights, Together against Poverty* is supporting millions of men, women, and children in their struggle to secure the rights they are currently denied, and bring an end to their poverty.

Central to the Campaign is Oxfam's Global Charter for Basic Rights, printed at the beginning of this book. As well as campaigns focusing on particular issues, such as Fair Trade or conflict, Basic Rights Hearings at national, regional, and local levels are aiming to put the whole issue of world poverty back on the moral and political agenda. These hearings are providing

MPs, campaigners, Oxfam staff, and some of the people Oxfam works with overseas, with a unique opportunity to address the need for basic rights, and to consider the consequences for people who are denied them. One end-result of the hearings will be a special report on world poverty, to be presented to the UK Parliament.

"The key message of the Campaign is very simple," says Simon Collings, a member of the co-ordinating group. "What we are saying is that poverty is wrong, and everyone has the responsibility to try to eradicate it. Over the next five years our aim is to make poverty as morally offensive as other human rights atrocities are today."

Above and opposite: Oxfam's Basic Rights Campaign is launched in Nottingham.

photo: Geoff Sayer

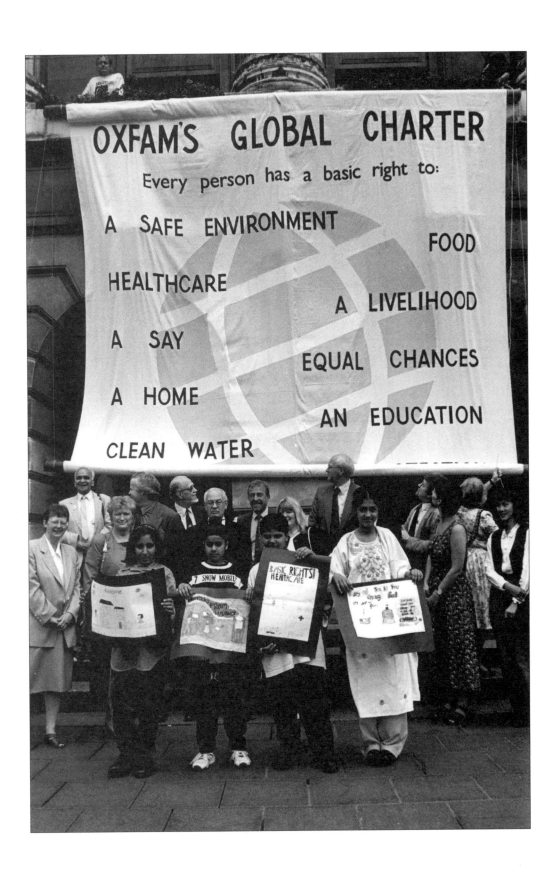

Universal Declaration of Human Rights

Adopted and proclaimed by General Assembly resolution 217 A (III) of 10 December 1948.

Preamble

Whereas recognition of the inherent dignity and of the equal and inalienable rights of all members of the human family is the foundation of freedom justice and peace in the world,

Whereas disregard and contempt for human rights have resulted in barbarous acts which have outraged the conscience of mankind, and the advent of a world in which human beings shall enjoy freedom of speech and belief and freedom from fear and want has been proclaimed as the highest aspiration of the common people,

Whereas it is essential, if man is not to be compelled to have recourse, as a last resort, to rebellion against tyranny and oppression, that human rights should be protected by the rule of law,

Whereas it is essential to promote the develop-ment of friendly relations between nations,

Whereas the peoples of the United Nations have in the Charter reaffirmed their faith in fundamental human rights, in the dignity and worth of the human person and in the equal rights of men and women and have determined to promote social progress and better standards of life in larger freedom,

Whereas Member States have pledged themselves to achieve, in cooperation with the United Nations, the promotion of universal respect for and observance of human rights and fundamental freedoms,

Whereas a common understanding of these rights and freedoms is of the greatest importance for the full realisation of this pledge,
Now, therefore, The General Assembly proclaims this Universal Declaration of Human Rights as a common standard of achievement for all peoples and all nations, to the end that every individual and every organ of society, keeping this Declaration constantly in mind, shall strive by teaching and education to promote respect for these rights and freedoms and by progressive measures, national and international, to secure their universal and effective recognition and observance, both among the people of Member States themselves and among the peoples of territories under their jurisdiction.

Article 1

All human beings are born free and equal in dignity and rights. They are endowed with reason and conscience and should act towards one another in a spirit of brotherhood.

Article 2

Everyone is entitled to all the rights and freedoms set forth in this Declaration, without distinction of any kind, such as race, colour, sex, language, religion, political or other opinion, national or social origin, property, birth or other status.

Furthermore, no distinction shall be made on the basis of the political, jurisdictional or international status of the country or territory to which a person belongs, whether it be independent, trust, non–self governing or under any other limitation of sovereignty.

Article 3

Everyone has the right to life, liberty and security of person.

Article 4

No one shall be held in slavery or servitude; slavery and the slave trade shall be prohibited in all their forms.

Article 5

No one shall be subjected to torture or to cruel, inhuman or degrading treatment or punishment.

Article 6

Everyone has the right to recognition everywhere as a person before the law.

Article 7

All are equal before the law and are entitled without any discrimination to equal protection of the law. All are entitled to equal protection against any discrimination in violation of this Declaration and against any incitement to such discrimination.

Article 8

Everyone has the right to an effective remedy by the competent national tribunals for acts violating the fundamental rights granted him by the constitution or by law.

Article 9

No one shall be subjected to arbitrary arrest, detention or exile.

Article 10

Everyone is entitled in full equality to a fair and public hearing by an independent and impartial tribunal, in the determination of his rights and obligations and of any criminal charge against him.

Article 11

1 Everyone charged with a penal offence has the right to be presumed innocent until proven guilty according to law in a public trial at which he has had all the guarantees necessary for his defence.

2 No one shall be held guilty of any penal offence on account of any act or omission which did not constitute a penal offence, under national or international law, at the time when it was committed. Nor shall a heavier penalty be imposed than the one that was applicable at the time the penal offence was committed.

Article 12

No one shall be subjected to arbitrary interference with his privacy, family, home or correspondence, nor to attacks upon his honour and reputation. Everyone has the right to the protection of the law against such interference or attacks.

Article 13

1 Everyone has the right to freedom of movement and residence within the borders of each State.

2 Everyone has the right to leave any country, including his own, and to return to his country.

Article 14

1 Everyone has the right to seek and to enjoy in other countries asylum from persecution.

2 This right may not be invoked in the case of prosecutions genuinely arising from non-political crimes or from acts contrary to the purposes and principles of the United Nations.

Article 15

1 Everyone has the right to nationality.
2 No one shall be arbitrarily deprived of his nationality nor denied the right to change his nationality.

Article 16

1 Men and women of full age, without any limitation due to race, nationality or religion, have the right to marry and to found a family. They are entitled to equal rights as to marriage, during marriage and at its dissolution.

2 Marriage shall be entered into only with the free and full consent of the intending spouses.

3 The family is the natural and fundamental group unit of society and is entitled to protection by society and the State.

Article 17

1 Everyone has the right to own property alone as well as in association with others.
2 No one shall be arbitrarily deprived of his property.

Article 18

Everyone has the right to freedom of thought, conscience and religion; this right includes freedom to change his religion or belief, and freedom, either alone or in community with others and in public or private, to manifest his religion or belief in teaching, practice, worship and observance.

Article 19

Everyone has the right to freedom of opinion and expression; this right includes freedom to hold opinions without interference and to seek, receive and impart information and ideas through any media and regardless of frontiers.

Article 20

1 Everyone has the right to freedom of peaceful assembly and association.

2 No one may be compelled to belong to an association.

Article 21

1 Everyone has the right to take part in the government of his country, directly or through freely chosen representatives.

2 Everyone has the right to equal access to public service in his country.

3 The will of the people shall be the basis of the authority of government; this will shall be expressed in periodic and genuine elections which shall be by universal and equal suffrage and shall be held by secret vote or by equivalent free voting procedures.

Article 22

Everyone, as a member of society, has the right to social security and is entitled to realisation, through national effort and international cooperation and in accordance with the organisation and resources of each State, of the economic, social and cultural rights indispensable for his dignity and the free development of his personality.

Article 23

1 Everyone has the right to work, to free choice of employment, to just and favourable conditions of work and to protection against unemployment.

2 Everyone, without any discrimination, has the right to equal pay for equal work.

3 Everyone who works has the right to just and favourable remuneration ensuring for himself and his family an existence worthy of human dignity, and supplemented, if necessary, by other means of social protection.

4 Everyone has the right to form and to join trade unions for the protection of his interests.

Article 24

Everyone has the right to rest and leisure, including reasonable limitation of working hours and periodic holidays with pay.

Article 25

1 Everyone has the right to a standard of living adequate for the health and well-being of himself and of his family, including food, clothing, housing and medical care and necessary social services, and the right to security in the event of unemployment, sickness, disability, widowhood, old age or other lack of livelihood in circumstances beyond his control.

2 Motherhood and childhood are entitled to special care and assistance. All children, whether born in or out of wedlock, shall enjoy the same social protection.

Article 26

1 Everyone has the right to education. Education shall be free, at least in the elementary and fundamental stages. Elementary education shall be compulsory. Technical and professional education shall be made generally available and higher education shall be equally accessible to all on the basis of merit.

2 Education shall be directed to the full development of the human personality and to the strengthening of respect for human rights and fundamental freedoms. It shall promote understanding, tolerance and friendship among all nations, racial or religious groups,

and shall further the activities of the United Nations for the maintenance of peace.

3 Parents have a prior right to choose the kind of education that shall be given to their children.

Article 27

1 Everyone has the right freely to participate in the cultural life of the community, to enjoy the arts and to share in scientific advancement and its benefits.

2 Everyone has the right to the protection of the moral and material interests resulting from any scientific, literary or artistic production of which he is the author.

Article 28

Everyone is entitled to a social and international order in which the rights and freedoms set forth in the Declaration can be fully realised.

Article 29

1 Everyone has duties to the community in which alone the free and full development of his personality is possible.

2 In the exercise of his rights and freedoms, everyone shall be subject only to such limitations as are determined by law solely for the purpose of securing due recognition and respect for the rights and freedoms of others and of meeting the just requirements of morality, public order and the general welfare in a democratic society.

3 These rights and freedoms may in no case be exercised contrary to the purposes and principles of the United Nations.

Article 30

Nothing in this Declaration may be interpreted as implying for any State, group or person any right to engage in any activity or to perform any act aimed at the destruction of any of the rights and freedoms set forth herein.

Campaign for Basic Rights
Campaign against Poverty

As we saw in chapter eight, Oxfam Campaigning is a diverse and dynamic force in the fight against global poverty. And the most important ingredient of campaigning is *people*.

If you're not already involved in the Oxfam Campaign

Join us today

Just write to Oxfam Operations Centre (WIA), 274 Banbury Road, Oxford OX2 7DZ, and say you wish to join the Oxfam Campaign. We'll send you an Action Pack.

Oxfam Publications

Oxfam (UK and Ireland) publishes a wide range of both manuals and resource materials for specialist, academic and general readers. The following titles may be of interest if you would like to know more about the issues discussed in *Words into Action*:

The Oxfam Poverty Report

Kevin Watkins
ISBN 0 85598 318 3
£9.95

No Time to Waste:
Poverty and the Global Environment

Joan Davidson and Dorothy Myers with Manab Chakraborty
ISBN 0 85598 183 0
£9.95

The Trade Trap:
Poverty and the Global Commodity Markets

Belinda Coote
ISBN 0 85598 135 0
£8.95

For further information on the full range of Oxfam Publications please write for a free catalogue to:
Oxfam Publishing, 274 Banbury Road, Oxford OX2 7DZ, UK